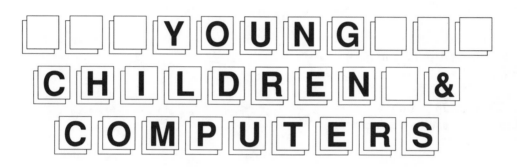

YOUNG CHILDREN & COMPUTERS

Related materials for educators and caregivers from the High/Scope Press:

Computer Learning for Young Children
Instructional Videotape

Extensions—
Newsletter of the High/Scope
Curriculum
(6 issues per year)

Survey of Early Childhood Software
(published annually)

The Teacher's Idea Book—
Daily Planning Around the Key
Experiences

Young Children in Action—
A Manual for Preschool Educators

Available from

THE HIGH/SCOPE® PRESS
A division of the
High/Scope Educational Research
Foundation
600 N. River Street
Ypsilanti, MI 48198-2898
(313) 485-2000
FAX (313) 485-0704

High/Scope also conducts computer training workshops for educators and caregivers. For information about the workshops, contact High/Scope's Development and Services Department at (313) 485-2000.

YOUNG CHILDREN & COMPUTERS

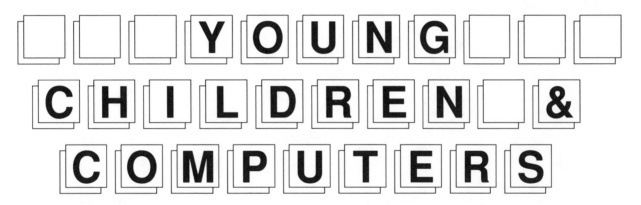

CHARLES HOHMANN

Coordinator of Curriculum
High/Scope Educational Research Foundation

THE HIGH/SCOPE® PRESS
Ypsilanti, Michigan

Published by
THE HIGH/SCOPE PRESS

A division of the
High/Scope Educational Research Foundation
600 North River Street
Ypsilanti, Michigan 48198-2898
(313)485-2000

Marge Senninger, High/Scope Press Editor

Linda Eckel, Graphic Designer

Gregory Fox, Photographer

Library of Congress Catalog Card Number:
LC 89-26703

ISBN 0-931114-24-1

Printed in the United States of America

10 9 8 7 6 5 4 3 2 1

The High/Scope Educational Research
Foundation is an independent nonprofit
organization formally established in 1970
by Dr. David P. Weikart. High/Scope is inter-
nationally known as a center for research,
curriculum development, professional
training, and public policy work. High/
Scope's work focuses on the learning and
development of children from infancy
through adolescence, with a special emphasis on the early childhood years.

Contents

Acknowledgments

Our most significant debt in learning about young children and computers is to the preschool and kindergarten children of the High/Scope demonstration classroom. We thank them and the numerous other preschoolers and kindergartners around the country whose teachers and caregivers have talked with us about their experiences using computers with young children. Though we had speculated a great deal about how young children might best use computers as a learning tool, about what software might work well, and about which configurations of equipment might be needed, tryouts with a range of children in a typically imperfect classroom setting periodically rewarded us with surprises: Some things worked that we had thought wouldn't; others that we had expected to work didn't, because of unanticipated "glitches"; and children often demonstrated computer learning outcomes we had not foreseen.

We owe thanks to many others who contributed to the development of this book. Warren Buckleitner, my co-worker in studying computer learning, located and previewed the computer programs we used. High/Scope Head Teacher Ruth Morrison Strubank, as someone new to computers, came to embrace them fully during the time that she accommodated our many needs for classroom tryouts of software and equipment. Her assistants over several years—Julie Ricks, Ann Rogers, Goranka Vukelich, Jenny Weikart, and Karl Wheatley—each added helpful insights about children's use of specific computer programs.

High/Scope President David Weikart and Executive Vice President Charles Wallgren vigorously supported the writing and publication of more than 30 issues of the computer newsletter *Key Notes*, which is where many of the topics in this book originated. Various other members of the High/Scope staff provided invaluable "reality checks" on our work, to keep the style and content of computer-related activities consistent with developmentally appropriate early childhood education. Finally, Marge Senninger's diligent editing contributed to the precision of our statements and to the coherence and comprehensiveness of our text.

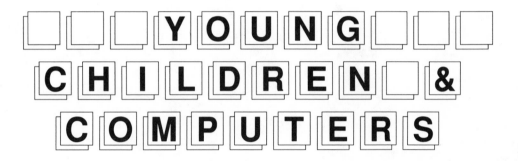

YOUNG CHILDREN & COMPUTERS

1 Introduction

Books about young children and books about computers are both easy to find. Books like this—ones *relating* the two topics—are not. This description of how young children and computers mix is the result of our observations over the past five years in the High/Scope demonstration classroom in Ypsilanti, Michigan.

Our book tells about young children of preschool and kindergarten age using computers to explore, create, and learn—and about adults planning for, supporting, and ultimately understanding the computer's proper role in young children's development. It is written for educators and caregivers who want to include, in the environments they create for young children, the learning resources available through computers. In addition, the book is for parents, program administrators, and public policymakers—anyone who is interested in critically examining the potential of computers for educating young children.

The growing use of computers in offices, factories, homes, and schools is often cited as a reason for introducing computers to children at ever earlier ages. Clearly, society (particularly a highly computerized society) can benefit from preparing its members to use computers. Whether young children, in particular those of preschool and kindergarten age, can benefit from an introduction to computers is another issue.

Our work studying the ways young children use computers and the ways their teachers use them has been a collective effort involving classroom teachers, curriculum developers, and other educators at the High/Scope Foundation. Initially charged to report on the possible contribution of the computer to the learning of young children within the framework of the High/Scope Curriculum, the curriculum developers gathered information about computer equipment and materials that related in any way to young children, reading everything available on the subject. At the same time, curriculum developers and teachers worked together to create a setting where children could try out the computer materials. A computer center, or area, was established within the High/Scope demonstration classroom. (In the demonstration classroom, two teachers work with 15–20 three- to six-year-old children of varied socioeconomic backgrounds, using a program based on the High/Scope Curriculum framework.) Throughout the past five years, the demonstration teachers, curriculum developers, and other staff at High/Scope have engaged in a continuing dialogue about the relationship of our computer work to the fundamental principles of the High/Scope Curriculum.

After completing our preliminary work identifying computer learning materials and after initiating computer activities at the demonstration center, we began sharing what we knew in training sessions with teachers and program directors across the country. Three years of training workshops have gradually brought us into contact with a great many other educators and caregivers who use computers with children of preschool and kindergarten age. Through the feedback they have given on our suggestions and through the questions and issues they have raised, these users have become part of the "we" used throughout this book. Our collective message is affirmative: **Young children can and do profit from computer activities if the activities suit the children's stage of development and are supported by appropriate adult assistance.** Moreover,

computer activities in preschool and kindergarten can result in active, independent, child-initiated learning, but this depends on the type of software used as well as on the way it is used. Finally, teachers from a variety of backgrounds, even those initially unfamiliar with computers, can embrace the computer both as a resource for children's learning and as a helpful tool for performing their own administrative tasks.

Central to High/Scope's study of children and computers has been our experience with early childhood programs and research. We have been early childhood educators first and computer enthusiasts second, asking each step of the way whether and how computers could assist both children and teachers in the teaching, learning, and organizing tasks common to most early childhood settings. **This perspective has led us to view the computer not as an end in itself—a new world for children to master—but as one more tool for children to use in discovering and mastering the world of familiar experience.**

In the High/Scope Curriculum, the computer is just one of the many classroom tools children use to discover and master the world of familiar experience.

We have been concerned with the computer as a tool for working with language; for discovering relationships of number and other kinds of quantity; and for exploring concepts of logic, space, and time—typical tasks for young children even before the advent of the computer. We have been less concerned, especially for the youngest children, with their knowledge of the computer itself—its parts and pieces, its programming, and its applications in banks, supermarkets, and factories. Viewing computers as a tool for early childhood learning, **our teachers have devised strategies whereby computer activities can support the autonomy of the child and facilitate the normal activities of early childhood classrooms; they have developed techniques that are comfortable for teachers and also in harmony with the social and emotional needs of young children.** The chapters that follow describe these strategies and techniques, which in our opinion, can make computer learning an effective and worthwhile part of a good preschool or kindergarten program. But first, a bit of background—

Computers Suited to Young Children: A Recent Development

The earliest microcomputers, those available in the late 1970s and early 1980s, were too limited in memory capacity and display capability to be used effectively by young children. (See the Glossary for definitions of *memory capacity, display capability,* and other specialized computer expressions.) Fashioned after their larger predecessors, these microcomputers were designed to work mainly with letters and numbers, highly symbolic material for most preschoolers. Furthermore, the computers could only produce line drawings or block pictures of low resolution—a far cry from what children see in books or on TV. These crude pictures were in monochrome only (white on black or green on black), and the limited memory capacity of the early micros meant that only a few such pictures (which require large chunks of memory) could be used in a given program.

Early micros, such as the Commodore PET, used cassette recorders and the associated cassette tapes to store programs. Loading a program into the computer meant playing a cassette tape into the computer—a process that could easily take several minutes each time the program was started. In our experience, young children were intolerant of such a wait. Waiting for a program to load from cassette, they sometimes began pounding the keyboard, demanding a response, or more often, they departed to find a more satisfying classroom activity. Also, operating the cassette recorders required pushing a series of keys in the proper order. Any sequence of two or more keystrokes seemed to be more than a four- or five-year-old could cope with.

By the early 1980s, however, when the Commodore 64 and Apple IIe computers first began appearing on the market, it was possible to buy a simple personal or home computer with vastly increased memory, color display capability, and fast disk drives for the storage and retrieval of programs. With these micros, programs could

Early micros, such as the Commodore PET, used cassette recorders and the associated cassette tapes to store programs.

load rapidly, incorporate numerous animated color pictures (a big improvement over the stick figures of earlier programs), and start not with keystrokes but with the computer's on/off switch. The advent of these features in microcomputers meant that earlier barriers to their use by young children were gone. Next, the question that arose was whether software designers would exploit these capabilities in programs *appropriate* for young children.

Software—A Key Element

Software programs are what bring a computer to life, enabling it to play a game, make musical sounds, or convert printed words into the speech of a talking robot. Thus, in beginning our study of the potential of young children's computer use, it seemed natural to begin with a look at the available software.

By 1985, the first year of our computer work with preschool and kindergarten children, Seymour Papert had already published *Mindstorms* (Basic Books, 1980), a seminal work describing how elementary school children used a computer program called LOGO. Using LOGO, children in Papert's lab wrote coded instructions to make a small floor robot, called a turtle, draw such shapes and figures as squares, triangles, and circles. In doing so, children could explore the properties of geometric shapes while also learning about the logical structures required in programming a computer. Papert's book and its strong advocacy of computers as *the* tool for children's learning tended to make LOGO synonymous with computer programs for children in the minds of many people; so it was to LOGO that we turned first in our study. Our investigation of work done by LOGO advocates, however, convinced us that no *one* program, such as a LOGO program, could provide the range of experiences suited to the emerging skills and interests of preschool and kindergarten children; multiple software programs would be needed.

A number of other computer programs aimed at young children had already been published by 1985, and many others were under development by educators and programmers working everywhere from basements to university laboratories. Therefore, our next undertaking was to study in detail this variety of rapidly evolving electronic literature.

The field of educational software, like that of children's literature, has spawned numerous authors, publishers, and critics. Many an entrepreneur has discovered the long and costly road from initial software ideas to profitable distribution of well-crafted programs. The result is a bewildering array of reviews, best sellers, awards, endorsements, and advertising. Since most users of classroom computers depend on commercially published materials rather than on homemade programs, we placed considerable emphasis on surveying the breadth and depth of the early childhood software market and identifying programs that are valuable for young children. (One outcome of this ongoing effort has been our annual publication of the *High/Scope Survey of Early Childhood Software*, which contains pertinent information covering virtually the full range of computer software designed for children of preschool and kindergarten age.)

Of course, new programs come, as new books do, each year. Fortunately, in this ever-expanding galaxy of software, we have found and continue to find good and useful programs for preschool and kindergarten classrooms. Experience using these programs has convinced us that **employing a variety of high-quality, age-appropriate software programs is the key to effective computer use with young children**.

The Questions That Guided Us

The underlying criteria throughout our investigation of the computer's potential for young children's learning have been those that in our view underlie effective early childhood programs in general. The foremost criterion for an effective early childhood learning program is the belief that **what is done for young children should be based on an early childhood curriculum that is grounded in a coherent child-development theory**. A developmental perspective such as this requires that early learning be something other than a watered-down version of what elementary school children are learning. Instead, the developmental early childhood program takes into consideration the child's processes for acquiring knowledge at various phases in development and builds on these. To judge the computer's "fit" with our developmental curriculum, we would need answers to several questions:

What Is the Computer's Social-Emotional Impact?

A major focus of our early childhood curriculum is children's social and emotional development, and we, like many educators, had concerns about the computer's possible negative impact on young children in these areas. For some people, this concern derives from images of youngsters as video game players or computer whizzes who have become absorbed in their computer activities to the exclusion of other kinds of stimulation and social interaction. Such fears are not without

foundation; computer activity can become powerfully absorbing, at least for some people. What social and emotional impacts computers would have in the preschool and kindergarten classroom was therefore an important question in our investigation of computer use with young children.

For preschoolers and kindergartners, it appears that the addition of computers and appropriate software to their environment has positive social consequences and does not disrupt other classroom social interactions. In other words, we have not seen young children becoming isolated "hackers." On the contrary, **we find that preschool children generally spend only 10 to 15 minutes at a time with a computer activity before moving on to something else, and they continue to find other classroom materials and activities of interest when computers are present**. Moreover, the computer in a preschool or kindergarten classroom can stimulate positive behaviors in children, like playing cooperatively and

The computer in a preschool or kindergarten classroom can stimulate children to play cooperatively and help one another.

helping one another. For example, children who experience success at the computer will often, by their enthusiasm, attract others to join them in the computer activity. Anxious to demonstrate their expertise, these "expert" children may offer to help other, more reticent children use the computer.

Computer activity can also provide some children with a much-needed boost in self-esteem, since it provides numerous opportunities for success. Sherry Turkle notes in *Computers and the Second Self* (Simon & Schuster, 1984) that for children who are already somewhat socially isolated, computer activity can provide a safe and successful experience that can be a first step to greater peer/adult interaction.

For certain children, the computer can be effective in promoting self-control. Impulsive children who have the urge to bang indiscriminately on the keys find that such outbursts are almost never rewarded by the sturdy and infinitely patient computer; much more satisfying results come from a more controlled pushing of individual keys in sync with the activities on the screen.

Generally, girls and boys of preschool to kindergarten age tend to use available computers with equal frequency and for similar durations. We suspect that early computer experiences for girls may, in fact, help to offset any later tendency for girls to defer to boys in the use of computers.[1]

Are Computer Experiences Too Symbolic for Young Children?

Our developmental perspective recognizes young children's preference for experiencing and learning directly, using all the senses. At the same time, we recognize their emerging ability to use symbols, even if they can only loosely connect symbolic systems like language, logic, numbers—even pictures—to direct, sensory experience. (Consider, for example, the fact that young children interact meaningfully with symbolic material they encounter in books read or shown to them by parents and other adults.) There is no question that the computer provides a symbolic rather than a direct learning experience. Therefore, on the pragmatic level, we wondered if children of preschool and kindergarten age could become engaged with the symbolic activities the computer offers—since this is a prerequisite for the computer's effectiveness as a learning tool. We also wondered whether the computer's symbolic activities would afford children significant learning that they could retain and also transfer to other, more direct, experiences.

We discovered that young children quite readily relate to computer-based learning materials. In addition to engaging enthusiastically in computer

---

[1]For more on sex differences regarding computer use, which appear to develop as children move into late elementary, junior, and senior high school, see John Lipkin and Linda McCormick, *Sex Bias at the Computer Terminal—How Schools Program Girls*, (NOW Legal Defense Fund, 1984), and J. A. Watson, R. E. Nida, and D. D. Shade, "Educational Issues Concerning Young Children and Microcomputers: Lego With LOGO?", *Early Child Development and Care, 23*, 299–316 (1986). A quote from the latter source: "Imagine what it might mean in the life of young girls to have positive early experiences with computers before society convinces them that 'computers are for boys.'"

We discovered that young children readily relate to computer-based learning materials, engaging enthusiastically in computer activities.

activities, children appear to learn from these activities in much the same way that they learn from other, non-computer activities. While our evaluation of the learning impact of young children's computer activities is far from definitive, there are more formal studies than ours that demonstrate clear-cut educational gains from computer experiences. (See Computer Effects in Kindergarten in Chapter 4.)

Is Computer Learning "Active Learning"?

Our developmental perspective also emphasizes the role of action in all learning, especially in the learning of young children. We initially questioned, therefore, whether computer learning is at all compatible with the notion of active learning. Compared with finger painting or a trip to the apple orchard, computer activities are certainly less physically active and less rich in sensory stimuli. Action, how-

The computer's capacity to create highly interactive settings leads to true "active learning" for children.

ever, doesn't have to be narrowly construed as involving such physical activity as touching, smelling, tasting, or "learning by doing." Though all of these contribute to active learning, action also includes the child's internal processes of transforming, comparing, organizing, and symbolizing—in short, the child's creation and consumption of knowledge.

We found that the computer's capacity to create highly interactive settings (like games, puzzles, and creative environments with accessible tools) gives it the potential to stimulate in young children the mental actions of transforming, comparing, organizing, and symbolizing. In this sense, then, computer learning *is* active learning.

Does the Computer Promote Child-Initiated Activity?

The belief that a curriculum should foster a high degree of child-initiated learning activity is another important aspect of our developmental perspective. This belief has been supported by recent research comparing the long-term effects of children's participation in different types of early childhood curricula. The research suggests that children who experience a high degree of choice and initiative in their preschool learning activities and become responsible for the outcomes of these activities gain significant educational and social benefits that reach well into their teen years.[2] Consequently, an-

[2]See L. J. Schweinhart, D. P. Weikart, and M. B. Larner, "Consequences of Three Preschool Curriculum Models Through Age 15," *Early Childhood Research Quarterly*, *1*, 15–45 (1986).

other question we asked ourselves was whether preschool and kindergarten computer learning could provide opportunities for child-initiated activity.

The answer to this question— a resounding yes—stems from our approach to the computer as a classroom "learning tool." Given the setup of the High/Scope classroom computer area and the thoughtful selection of computer programs, once our teachers introduce a computer activity to children (as they would introduce any other new learning tool or material), children's involvement in the activity tends to be highly independent. In fact, once children become familiar with operating the computer, computer activities often require even less teacher support than many other kinds of classroom activities require. When children have a variety of familiar programs to choose from (and these may range from highly open-ended to quite structured), children not only choose the particular programs they will use but also make many choices as they work through each program (providing it is well designed). From program initiation to completion, a child can truly feel in control of his or her own computer learning.

What Role Do Adults Play?

In addition to questions stemming from our developmental perspective on early childhood education, we also had some organizational questions regarding the teacher's role in classroom computer learning. Would computers, as had frequently been claimed, help relieve the tedium of such tasks as

keeping records, preparing reports, ordering supplies, and allow teachers to focus their energies on the more creative aspects of teaching? In what ways could teachers support the computer learning activities?

To no one's surprise, we have found that classroom computers are not miracle workers that will relieve teachers of every burden; they are not the handy robots we may have imagined mixing paints or wiping tables for us; nor are they the ultimate in teaching machines—technological wizards that will give every child the IQ of a genius. Neither, however, do computers create special burdens for teachers.

For some types of activities—children's beginning writing activities, for example—a computerized approach actually requires less adult involvement than a noncomputerized approach would require. Classroom computers *with well-chosen software* can provide eventful situations that young children can interact with largely on their own. To the extent that computer programs *engage* children in extended creative problem solving and thinking, they are the teacher's friend and ally—a teaching-learning resource that simulates a teacher's attention by responding selectively to children's actions.

We were also uncertain of the role that parents might play at home in arranging and supervising computer activities for young children. There were, in 1985, predictions afoot that school as we know it might disappear, since computers could provide essential instruction at home, and that school might embrace totally different tasks, such as field trips and group projects—learning activities involving social interaction.

We discovered very quickly that while High/Scope's parents were highly sup-

Classroom computers with well-chosen software *provide learning situations that young children can deal with largely on their own.*

portive of computer learning for their children in school, most could not follow up with computer activities at home, simply because most homes did not have computers. Obviously, no efforts to link school computer learning with similar efforts at home can go very far until home computers are as universal as television sets. Any projects studying the effects of home computer learning usually provide families with the needed computers. As one would expect, such studies often find pronounced benefits to children when homes have computers and computer use is coordinated between home and school.

Looking Ahead

These have been some of the guiding questions in our exploration of computers. The succeeding chapters of this book expand on the brief answers we have already given to the questions raised here. Chapter 2 will help you get started with classroom computers—advising you about what equipment and materials to buy and how to make it all accessible to children. Chapter 3 outlines the possible uses of the computer throughout a typical day in the preschool or kindergarten classroom. The two chapters following that describe specific computer programs promoting young children's language development and logical/mathematical thinking. The concluding chapter addresses other significant curriculum issues involved in young children's computer use.

② The Computer: What to Buy, Where to Put It

Getting started with computer learning for children of preschool and kindergarten age involves selecting suitable computer equipment, or **hardware**, and appropriate programs, or **software**. This chapter provides selection guidelines to help assure you a successful start. Of course, the amount and type of hardware and software you select is greatly dependent on the kind of setting you want to create for children's computer learning.

Why Not a Lab Setting?

Throughout this book, we take the position that the most appropriate location for computers in preschool or kindergarten is in the classroom rather than in a separate computer lab. Locating computers in a lab seems to us to emphasize the importance of the computer itself. **For young children, the computer is only important as part of the larger learning environment of the classroom—as one of many choices in an environment that encourages children to initiate and choose activities.** Thus, while a separate computer lab may have some strategic advantages (such as spreading a school's computer investment over more children and perhaps providing the expertise of a lab teacher), we found that the advantages of integrating the computer into the classroom outweighed the advantages of locating it in a lab.

With one or more computers located in **a computer area within the classroom**, computer activities can be readily coordinated with other classroom activities. Children come to accept the computer area as one of a variety of work areas available to them, and it becomes a center of social interaction where children share, take turns, help one another, and communicate purposefully. In short, computer learning—if it is skillfully integrated into the classroom—can reflect and support an open-ended learning environment that encourages child-initiated activity.

Planning the Classroom Computer Area

A computer area should contain all the equipment and materials needed for computer use. Like the other work areas of the classroom, it should be

■ **Defined** with shelves or other dividers, so children have a sense of being in a distinct area of the room.

■ **Built with shelves or dividers low enough** to allow children in the computer area to see out and others to see in.

■ **Designed to be accessible throughout**, so equipment and support materials meant to be used by children are easy to see and reach.

■ **Equipped with a display area** for children's computer work.

■ **Labeled** with a sign saying "computer area." Labels should also identify equipment ("computer," "monitor," "keyboard").

A computer area should contain all the equipment and materials needed for children's computer use.

To define the computer area, start with sturdy, low, trapezoid-shaped tables with adjustable legs. The trapezoidal classroom tables available from school and office supply companies are fine for this purpose and are less expensive than special computer tables. If you have, for example, three classroom computers, arrange three such tables—one for each computer—in a semicircle in a corner of the room to create a cozy and functional area that can serve three to six children working singly or in pairs. Place a computer on each table, with the monitors' screens facing towards the center of the semicircle. This arrangement encourages helping and sharing among children but also helps children focus on separate screen activities when necessary. Such an arrangement also permits one adult to see all the screens at once, when the adult is working with the children or checking to see if some child needs help.

Some additional design considerations are unique to a work area intended for computer use. For example, be sure that your computer area

■ Has chairs and tables that allow monitors to be at a child's eye-level and keyboards to be at a child's elbow-height

■ Has at least one shelf out of children's reach, for storage of hard-to-replace fragile materials, such as back-up copies of program disks (discussed later in this chapter)

■ Is located so that windows and lights do not create undue glare or reflection on the monitor screens

■ Has all wires and plugs well out of children's reach

If the computer area is backed up against a corner of the room, as we have described, wires and cables attached to the rear of computers, monitors, and power packs should not be a safety hazard any more than those of other audiovisual equipment, such as a record player or tape recorder. We found that young children quickly adapted to having power cords nearby and understood that they were off-limits.

We've described an arrangement of three computers and monitors, but just one computer and monitor can satisfactorily equip a preschool or kindergarten computer area. We'll mention the necessary amount of equipment again when we address the question of hardware choices, later in the chapter. Also, when we suggest ways to integrate the computer into the classroom routine (in Chapter 3), you may get a better idea of how much equipment you want. Before talking about choosing hardware, however, we'd like to recommend some helpful extra features for your computer area.

One feature is having a **computer cart** available—one with wheels and height-adjustment. This is useful for moving a computer from the work area to another part of the room—as you might do, for example, for small-group or circle activities.

The other recommended feature is a **"computer's-on beacon."** Because of the small size of the computer equipment's indicator lights, a computer can accidentally be left on at night or over the weekend; it's happened in our classroom and it could in yours. It's OK to forget to turn off the equipment

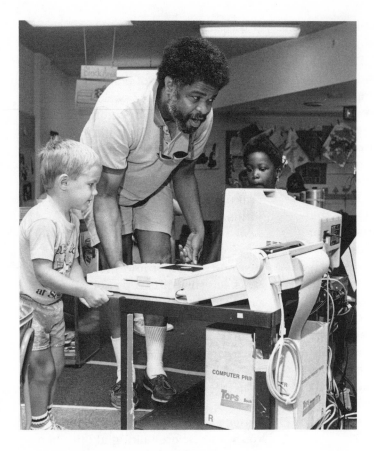

A computer cart is useful for moving a computer from the work area to another part of the room, for example, for small-group or circle activities.

once in a while; since it uses just a small amount of electricity, the cost of leaving it on is minimal. But if you repeatedly forget to turn it off, your forgetfulness can shorten the computer's life, cause it to overheat, or expose it to damaging electrical currents caused by lightning from electrical storms (even when you use a surge protector).

Here's a tip to help you avoid such disasters: Hang a small lamp, a droplight, or a night-light on an extension cord in a conspicuous place above the computer area. This can act as your "computer's-on beacon." Simply plug the computer equipment and the light into a power strip (a box with five or six outlets and a switch) to provide power for your entire computer area. Leaving the light and all the individual

equipment switches on, you can use just the single switch on the power strip to turn all the computer equipment off at the end of the day, when a glance at the beacon reminds you to do so.

Now, with this vision of your computer area in mind, you'll need to make some decisions about what equipment and materials to buy.

Essentials: A Computer and a Screen

Computer equipment for use with children three to six years of age should include, as a minimum, **a computer with one floppy disk drive and standard memory capacity, plus a color monitor**. (Standard memory capacity is

Plugging all your computer equipment into a power strip makes it possible to use a single switch to turn all the computer equipment off at the end of the day.

at least 128K for Apple II and compatible computers, 64K for Commodore computers, and 256K for IBM and compatible computers.)

One floppy disk drive is sufficient for operating virtually every program for young children. Some programs are available on the newer 3½-inch disks, but many are not, so we recommend the larger 5¼-inch drive, especially for Apple and Commodore computers. If you are planning a system with two disk drives, even though this is not necessary, one 5¼-inch drive and a second drive of the 3½-inch variety will allow your computer to accommodate floppy disks of either size.

Most programs for young children will work on a computer with **standard memory capacity**, though a few require more. The memory capacity of a computer determines how much of a program can be placed in the computer's memory at one time and hence how fast and efficient program operation is.

A **color monitor** is essential for young children, since most worthwhile early childhood programs use color as a device in presenting concepts and menu choices. The color monitor you

select can be the simplest type, the **composite color monitor**, in which all the colors are created by one electron gun in the picture tube. More expensive, and usually larger, is the more sophisticated **RGB monitor**. (The acronym signifies that it has separate red, green, and blue electron guns in the picture tube.) An RGB monitor is not necessary for early childhood use unless you are planning to use your computer for your own word processing. In this case, you will need a monitor capable of displaying 80 small letters, or characters, per line across the screen, and the RGB does this best.

Historically, computers with more and more advanced features have gradually become available for less and less money, and this trend is very likely to continue. In such a rapidly changing environment, specific equipment recommendations may quickly become outdated. While we are aware of this potential problem, the broad suggestions we give here have remained valid for several years and will, we believe, remain so for some years to come. We have tried to recommend serviceable systems for young children—ones that should become increasingly cost-effective over time if the "more for less" trend continues.

Which System Should You Choose?

The availability of good software is the most important criterion to consider in selecting a computer system. Not all early childhood software is available for all machines. Programs written for one machine usually cannot be run on another. Therefore **your choice of computer hardware should be based on the software you want to use with it**.

The *High/Scope Survey of Early Childhood Software* (Buckleitner, High/Scope Press, 1989) indicates that 307 early childhood software programs are available for Apple II computers (and for the compatible Laser computers). Though not all 307 programs are developmentally appropriate or easy for young children to use, most of the good early childhood programs are included in this number.

The *High/Scope Survey* ranks the Commodore 64/128 computer second in software availability (124 programs). Like the Apple II series, the Commodore line has been around for many years, so there is a long list of good early childhood programs available for Commodores. Commodore has recently introduced a remodeled version of the C64, which indicates the company's commitment to the product for the foreseeable future and a continuing market for new programs for the machine.

Ranked third in early childhood software availability is the IBM (this also includes the IBM-compatible machines, such as the Tandy 1000 series and clones of the original IBM-PC by Zenith, Epson, and others). The *High/Scope Survey* lists 115 early childhood programs available for the IBM. IBM computers and IBM compatibles have historically been the computers of choice for business use, though Apple's Macintosh computers have more recently made a strong bid for a share of the business market. Currently, price competition among the IBM-compatible equipment has driven machine prices (and even the prices of color systems needed to run these programs) down to historic lows.

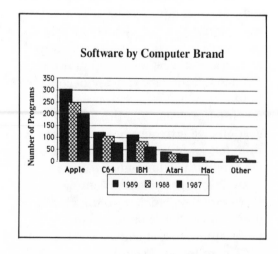

Source: Warren Buckleitner, High/Scope Survey of Early Childhood Software (Ypsilanti, MI: High/Scope Press, 1989).

What's Our Pick for Most Cost-Effective Starter Machine?

Apple IIe or Apple IIGS (or the Apple-compatible Laser 128), with one 5¼-inch disk drive and a composite color monitor, is our choice for relatively low-cost equipment to use with young children, because of the range of useful and appropriate early childhood software that is available for any of these machines. Another consideration influencing our pick is that the IIGS includes improved sound and graphics, a mouse, and a printer hookup.

Thus, on the basis of software availability, any one of the computer brands just mentioned would be a reasonable choice for early childhood use. Though Apple II computers (see box) clearly have the largest supply of young children's software, the Commodore 64 offers the least expensive choice. Also, IBM and compatible computers have the advantage of providing many business applications. You should be aware, too, that newer IBM models (such as the Model 25) are aimed at the education market and have revived software publishers' interest in producing educational programs for IBM computers.

There are a number of other computers on the market, such as Apple's Macintosh, Commodore's Amiga, other Tandy models, Atari models. Although these machines offer many exciting features, the amount of useful early childhood software currently available for them is quite small—not enough to provide a worthwhile range of experiences for preschoolers and kindergartners. Therefore we recommend that you avoid these machines unless you are particularly interested in them and can provide a variety of programs of your own design.

Selecting hardware for early childhood computer learning can be a complicated task when you are trying to obtain equipment that fits a budget, provides a suitable range of applications now, and is not likely to be left behind as new technology is introduced. However, we feel that the standard Apples, Commodores, and IBMs will most likely be in use for a number of years.

Peripherals, Some More Necessary Than Others

Once you have the computer, disk drive, and monitor, you have the basics you need for classroom computer activities: The computer's keyboard allows children to enter information (input), and the monitor allows children to receive information (output). The possibilities are many for adding "bells and whistles"—additional input or output devices—to your classroom computer system. Common sense and your expanding experience with programs will tell you when and if any of the extras (called peripherals) we describe here are needed to meet the needs of your preschool or kindergarten children.

We find some of the following peripherals to be virtually essential to our children for their daily computer use. Others are necessary only if we wish to use certain worthwhile programs. One or two others are novelties but easy to do without.

Output Devices

If you want computer output that is tangible, you might consider adding a printer to your basic system. For audible output, you will need to add a speech synthesizer. Adding one or both of these output devices increases the benefits children can gain from their computer activities.

Printers add concreteness. The output device our preschoolers and kindergartners use most frequently—daily, in fact—is a printer. The **printer** allows characters or images from the computer screen or information on a computer disk to be printed on paper. With a printer, children can use the computer (with certain programs) to produce typed words or sentences and to generate pictures or drawings on paper. In other words, the printer can make a permanent copy of work accomplished on the computer screen. Of course, printing capability is central to writing (word processing) programs and to programs for making drawings, masks, cutouts, banners, and signs. When children use such computer programs, having a concrete, portable product to show for their labors gives them special satisfaction. This printed product can help them follow through

on a computer activity with related projects in other areas of the classroom and at home. It can also help them recall and explain their work to others.

A printer can benefit the teacher as well. Teachers in our classroom use the printer to write letters to parents; to write up student evaluations; to tabulate information about budgets, plans, and materials; and to produce such classroom materials as signs, labels, and child-dictated stories.

Which printer should you choose? Choice of a printer, like choice of a computer, depends on what software you want to use. This is because, to print, each program must tell the computer how to carry out the printing task—and these instructions vary for different printers; so most programs that require use of a printer, whether for letters and words or for pictures and drawings, will contain a special menu of printer options to set the program up to work with any of the most common printers. Then, once you have chosen your printer's name from this menu, the program and printer will be set up to work together.

Ideally then, before buying a printer, you should check the software programs you're hoping to use, to see which printers are listed on their printer setup menus. If this is not possible, you will generally be safe in selecting one of the most popular printers or one of those produced by your computer's manufacturer. Apple, for example, sells the Imagewriter II printer that is designed to work with its II+, IIe, and IIc computers; Commodore provides several printers designed to work with the Commodore

An output device children use frequently is a printer— and using a scissors to remove the printed product from the printer seems to work best for many children.

computers; likewise, IBM produces printers for its computers. Basic printers are all of the dot matrix variety (which form images as a pattern of pin-sized dots), capable of printing standard number and letter characters as well as pictures and drawings.

Some, such as the Apple Imagewriter II and the IBM Color Graphics printer, print in color—a desirable feature for young children's programs. The dot matrix printers, including the color ones, are of relatively low cost ($200–$500) and are sturdy and reliable. In addition, a number of other companies, like Epson, Okidata, and Star Micronics, manufacture similarly capable dot matrix color printers for about $200–$300.

Most programs work with the most common computers and printers, but no flat statement can be made about any one printer working for all programs or for most programs. Still, we can say with relative assurance that most programs for Apple computers will work with Imagewriter, Epson, and Okidata printers. If you are going to use a printer with a variety of programs for early childhood, it is best to buy one of the standard printers, such as one of those indicated in the previous paragraph.

While we're on the subject of printers, we think it worth mentioning the printer **T-switch**, which allows one printer to serve more than one computer. With this switch, more than one printing program (perhaps a drawing and a writing program) can be used at the same time by different children on different computers. The switch enables the printer to print for either program. A T-switch can be either manual or automatic, but we recommend the automatic T-switch for use with young children, so that the timing of the printer's switching is automatic and not disruptive to printer or computers. Such a switch can, for example, put "on hold" a second computer that is trying to print, while a first computer finishes printing.

"Snapshots" aid recall. So far, we've talked about printing results of programs *designed* to give printed output,

such as word-processing or drawing programs. But for the many programs not designed to give printed results, the picture or text that appears on the screen when the program is operating is useful to a child for the moment but lost as soon as the machine is turned off. Thus there is nothing tangible that the child can use to describe or recall the screen experience. Taking a Polaroid snapshot of the screen would be one way to capture the experience, but there's another device, called a **screen dump**, that will do the job.

A screen dump is an output device that at the push of a button or key, enables the printer to capture on paper what appears on the monitor's screen at any given moment. With some computers, the Apple IIe for example, you'll need a special screen dump attachment to do this (such as Fingerprint by Thirdware Computer Products). IBM and most IBM compatible computers come with a built-in PRINT SCREEN key (labeled "PrtSc") that with the aid of appropriate software accomplishes the same task. Whether the screen dump is attached or built in, you of course need a printer to use it. Though the screen dump is certainly not essential, the device can be a classroom asset because it gives children a tangible result from *any* kind of program they might use.

Speech enhances interaction. Though monitors and printers are the most common devices used for computer output, devices that provide spoken output are increasing in popularity, particularly for use with young children who cannot read. Called **speech synthesizers**, these devices allow the computer to generate speech sounds and, with the proper software, to convert letters and words to speech. This feature greatly increases the possibilities for computer-child interaction

A screen dump from Richard Scarry's Best Electronic Word Book Ever!

A screen dump from Mask Parade

and has particular promise for helping children learn to read and write. More and more software products that rely on speech synthesis are becoming available, and these are aimed at children of preschool and kindergarten age. Later in this book, we will discuss some of these programs in more detail.

Input Devices

The computer you select will have a standard keyboard that a child or adult can use to enter information and thus control the computer. Most computers also permit the use of alternate control, or input, devices. The development of alternatives to the standard-keyboard method of input has received particular emphasis with the handicapped, since special input devices can help them overcome limitations of speech or movement, or other disabilities. Alternate input devices have also proved useful to the nonhandicapped. For certain programs—some of them aimed at

young children—a control like the mouse, joystick, or touchpad is the preferred input device. Of course, each of these input methods has its advantages and disadvantages.

Intuitive and speedy methods. Children in our classroom make most frequent use of two nonkeyboard methods of input—the **joystick** and the **mouse**. Each of these is a device that the child can move to direct a cursor's (or pointer's) movement on the screen. For example, pushing the joystick forward moves the cursor to the top of the screen; pulling back on the joystick moves the cursor to the bottom of the screen. Similarly, moving the mouse on a flat surface forward, backward, to the left, or to the right moves the screen's cursor up, down, left, or right. This, of course requires the child to link the joystick or mouse movement to the cursor movement, which takes some practice. We find that most three- and four-year-old children, using trial and error, can master this skill in a few short practice sessions.

For computer drawing activities, both mouse and joystick are superior to a keyboard. In fact, serious drawing programs *require* either the mouse or joystick. Joysticks most readily move the cursor up/down or left/right and thus are good for straight-line drawings. Using a mouse, children find it easier to draw curves than to draw straight lines.

Children can also use a joystick or mouse to point to choices displayed on the computer screen, as they might do in selecting a set of dog bones to match one-to-one with a set of dogs, for example. However, the young child's manual dexterity is an issue in using a joystick or mouse for pointing or menu selection; stopping the joystick or mouse movement precisely when the screen's cursor is on the intended target may be difficult. Overshooting a targeted menu choice may give the

Most three- and four-year-old children, using trial and error, can master the skill of using a joystick in a few short practice sessions.

One advantage of the mouse seems to be its intuitive appeal to the child—hand movement producing similar on-screen movement.

child an unintended choice, which can be mystifying and frustrating (even to some adults). So for menu selection, children may prefer to use the arrow keys, which move the cursor in gradual, discrete steps to the intended target.

The advantages of the mouse and joystick seem to be their intuitive appeal to the child (hand movement producing screen movement), their

speedy results (as opposed to the small, incremental movements made by using the arrow keys), and their portability (making it easy to pass them around when taking turns at controlling a computer activity).

Input by touch. Two other non-keyboard devices, both making use of touch, are the **Touch Window** (by Edmark Corporation) and the **Koala Pad** (by PTI/Koala Industries). These were used only infrequently in our classroom, for a handful of programs that permitted their use.

The **Touch Window** is a transparent panel about the size of a small TV screen. The panel attaches to a monitor's screen by means of adhesive Velcro strips. Used with certain computer programs, the panel makes the screen sensitive to the touch of a finger or soft pointer. For example, with the Touch Window on the screen, a child might point to an object to indicate that it is different from several others displayed on the screen, or the child might move a finger or pointer across the Touch Window and thus draw on the screen. This device also allows the child to select a menu item by simply pointing to it on the screen.

The Touch Window can be used in another way. Given a printed sheet corresponding to the material appearing on the screen, a child can also use the Touch Window by placing it over the printed sheet and then doing the pointing or drawing on this surface. Some programs supply printed sheets to be used with the Touch Window in this way. For young children, or anyone with fine-motor control difficulties, the Touch Window might be a particularly useful device, one they find easier to use than the keyboard.

The other input device relying on touch, the **Koala Pad**, is a notebook-sized pad that allows a child to enter information into the computer by drawing on the pad with a finger or stylus. Only a few drawing programs use the Koala Pad. One drawback is the pad's small size and the tendency of children, while using the Koala Pad, to forget about the screen and concentrate only on the pad. The Touch Window, being transparent and fitting over the screen, does not have this "distraction factor."

A simplified keyboard. An input device that was specially designed for young children is a simplified keyboard called **Muppet Learning Keys** (by Sunburst Communications, Inc.). It is a brightly colored 14 × 14-inch durable plastic board with letter keys arranged in alphabetical order and with number keys from 0 to 9 arranged in left-to-right order (recall that a standard keyboard places 0 out of order, to the right of 9). This substitute for the standard keyboard plugs into the joystick port of Apple, IBM, and Commodore computers. It is mobile because it is lightweight and connected to the computer by a long cord—as an IBM or Apple IIGS keyboard is. (Other Apple II and Commodore keyboards are built into the computer.)

On the Muppet board, special-purpose keys have child-oriented names and pictures to suggest their function. For example, the standard ENTER (or RETURN) key is labeled "GO" on the Muppet board. To erase the last character typed, an OOPS key serves as the equivalent of the standard DELETE key. An ERASER key (with a picture of an eraser) clears the screen; a HELP key retrieves help messages (if they are available); a paint-box array of color keys select the color of the display; and a ZAP key (acting as the standard ESCAPE key) stops the activity and returns to the menu or beginning.

The Muppet keyboard's bright colors, mobility, and pictures give it more child-appeal than the standard keyboard. Also, the arrangement of the numbers—in order, with 0 at the left—is in keeping with number-ordering concepts children will be learning. Likewise, the alphabetical arrangement of letters will jibe with their learning alphabetical order. But even when children *do* know something of alphabetical order, searching for specific letters on the Muppet keyboard seems to be just as time-consuming as searching for them on the standard keyboard. In fact, in most computer activities, children seem to succeed with the standard keyboard as well as they do with the Muppet keyboard. Furthermore, since only a small fraction of the software for young children uses Muppet Learning Keys, children will most likely have to adapt to the standard keyboard for other programs available in the classroom.

We find young children to be remarkably adept at using the standard keyboard in their computer activities. Fortunately, most programs for young children are designed so they require the use of only a few of the standard keys in the program's operation. For example, many programs use just the spacebar, RETURN (or ENTER) key, and ESCAPE key. To aid children in finding these vital keys, you might highlight them with strips of tape or colorful stickers.

To Buy or Not to Buy?

We have not tried to describe in this chapter every possible computer choice and all the available peripherals. Rather, we have focused on equipment that is most likely to be appropriate for young children and that is currently available at reasonable cost. Your choice of additional input and output devices will depend on the specific activities you want to introduce (such as writing, drawing) and the equipment requirements of the programs you want to use. Since relative costs might also influence your buying decisions, Table 1 gives approximate costs of the peripherals we've described in this chapter.

Table 1

Approximate Peripheral Costs[a]

Input/Output Device	Cost
Printer (basic dot matrix)	$200–500
T-switch for printer	100
Screen dump	100[b]
Speech synthesizer	100–150
Joystick	25–50
Mouse	50–100
Touch Window	200
Koala Pad	70
Muppet Learning Keys	100

[a]Educational discounts of up to 30 percent are usually available. Mail-order catalogs usually offer the best prices. Look for their ads in the back pages of computer magazines.

[b]Built in on most IBM and IBM-compatible computers.

Just as youngsters strive to outdo their peers with the bells and whistles they add to their bicycles, so computer owners are fond of adding the latest gizmos to their machines. The array of memory expansions, disk drives, and printers that can be added to basic systems grows daily. While many of these additions can truly improve the capabilities of a basic system, few of these improvements make sense for early childhood use. Another consideration that argues against such additions is that complex systems can require someone skilled in keeping them running smoothly.

The basic, stand-alone computer system we've described in this chapter (that is, a system including monitor, disk drive, and possibly printer) requires essentially one-step operation. You turn the computer on—and go! Careful initial selection of computer equipment will result in a simple and workable system for everyday classroom use but also keep the door open for future expansion.

As we have said more than once, the software you intend to use will be a key factor in your choice of hardware. The next section treats the subject of software, giving guidelines for evaluating and choosing worthwhile computer programs.

Selecting Software

Faced with the task of making the very best selection from the large array of early childhood programs available, educators often feel overwhelmed. Making the task even more mind-boggling are the ever-changing fads and fashions of the software market, which leave the consumer feeling that something new and better is just about to be announced. If you don't succumb to the hype, however, the job of selecting software can be a lot easier. Most educators' expectations about software are just too high. Believing that software is as good as the advertising says it is almost always leads to disappointment and adds to the frenzy of searching high and low for the best. Here are a few guidelines that can help you establish realistic expectations for early childhood software:

The first consideration in selecting software should be your educational objectives. **Start your search with learning goals in mind.** Are you seeking a program containing number or language concepts? Then don't be seduced by software that you like for some other reason but that does not carry its weight as a learning tool. It's easy to forget content when looking at programs, because the colors, characters, animation, and other features can be so appealing and attention grabbing.

Once you've defined your learning goals, you can easily **establish a realistic number of programs to look for**. The objectives of your early childhood program probably cover learning in a half-dozen or so subject areas, such as language, number, spatial relations, and time concepts. Finding one or two programs in each of five or six such areas is a realistic and balanced expectation.

You'll also make your search easier if you **try to be realistic about what software can do**. Computers do many clever things, but don't expect miracles. Computer programs have many limitations, as does any learning tool.

For example, the pictures and sounds generated by a computer program are substantially different from the pictures and sounds of a TV program. And computer programs don't produce special effects comparable to those seen in movies.

Finally, **don't expect computer software to do your work for you**. Realize that the computer is, at best, an aid to teaching, not a replacement for the teacher. Be ready to supplement each computer program with activities that introduce the program to children and activities that follow up on the program. Preschool and kindergarten children need adult help to benefit from computer materials.

Caring for Your Software Disks

Software programs are recorded on the magnetic surfaces of floppy disks. These disks are vulnerable to damage from improper handling, so adults and children should observe the following cautions:

■ **Keep the disks flat** and avoid bending them, especially as they are being inserted into the disk drive. A crease can prevent a disk from turning properly in the disk drive.

■ **Hold the disk along the edges** to keep from touching the open slot where the recording surface is exposed. Fingerprints, peanut butter, or other foreign matter in this area can damage the recorded material or make it unreadable.

■ **Keep the disks away from things that may become magnetized**—telephones, scissors, staplers—any steel objects (large metal surfaces such as carts or tables are usually okay).

■ **Keep back-up copies of your program disks in a location not accessible to children.** Many software publishers provide back-up copies in standard software packages. Others do so for an additional cost that is usually a fraction of the package purchase-price. Still others will replace a damaged program disk for a small fee if the original is returned. Programs are available for making your own back-up copy of a program (a process permitted under current software copyright laws unless back-ups are provided with the original), but these programs cannot be counted on to copy *every* program.

A Checklist for Quality

Once you've used the guidelines just mentioned to narrow the field and bring expectations down to a realistic level, you can evaluate individual preschool and kindergarten software programs with the following checklist of desirable qualities:

■ **Easy to use**—The program should start as soon as the computer is turned on, or the program should begin with a simple picture menu. Program formats should require the child to use only one key at a time. Instructions should be limited and at the child's level.

■ **Interactive**—The best programs are ones that require frequent reactions, decisions, or creative input from the child.

■ **Childproof**—The designers of good software know that children will experiment with all the keys. Good programs can handle busy fingers and an occasional elbow without "locking up."

■ **Designed with features for teachers and parents**—Look for codes adults can use to control the sound, add new challenges, or review what a child has done while using the program. Well-designed programs give adults such options and have clear written instructions describing the options.

■ **Strong in content**—If you can't put your finger on the learning content, it's probably weak. Worthwhile programs give the feeling that they're about something: shapes, words, patterns, classification, numbers.

■ **Child-controlled**—A program should never leave the child feeling trapped into continuing to the end of an activity. It should be easy for the child to pause, finish up quickly, go on to another level of activity, or stop altogether (for example, the ESCAPE key often provides a quick and easy way out of an activity).

■ **Designed to aid learning**—Clear pictures and interesting sounds related to the learning activity—not just fanfares of color and sound—are signs of a good program. Programs that offer novelty each time they are used and provide feedback on success and failure are superior. Consider also programs that automatically adjust themselves to a child's performance, moving down a level to help the child who repeatedly makes mistakes and moving up a level for a child ready for a greater challenge.

If a program has most of the qualities we've just listed, there's a good chance that children will both benefit from it and enjoy using it. Our quality checklist was distilled from a much more detailed software feature checklist used by High/Scope evaluators to systematically review and rate software presently available for young children. While no evaluation process can be completely unbiased, it was the aim of the High/Scope reviewers to be as objective as possible in cataloging, describing, and ranking programs. Their results are published in the annual *High/Scope Survey of Early Childhood Software* that we have mentioned earlier.

Software Reviews

Much of today's software evaluation is done as High/Scope's was, by a checklist method. This is because data ranking educational software on the basis of demonstrated long-term results are too scarce and too difficult and costly to collect. Recently, however, a few studies have assessed program effectiveness, and additional research information will no doubt be collected as computer use widens. Meanwhile, the process of choosing software is somewhat like the process you might use to choose which make of car to buy—reading reviews, asking advice of users, and checking certain features firsthand.

When using reviews of one form or another in your selection of software, remember that the reviewing process may be somewhat subjective; reviews often reflect the teaching experience of the reviewer, or the audience to which they are directed. They may or may not be the results of close scrutiny, such as some systematic checklist procedure or classroom tryouts with children. The software recommendations we make in this book are based on both our checklist evaluations and our classroom tryouts.

Some software producers have a 30-day preview policy to allow you to try out programs before finalizing your purchase. If you preview a program in this way, be warned that even software chosen on the best of recommendations from reviewers or users may *initially* fall flat in your classroom. In this case, patience and repeated use may prove to be the answer. We found the second or third use of a program was likely to be better than the first. Computers and their software are only tools for learning—and even the best tools are most effective when users have some training and practice.

Starter Sets of Software

If you can afford just a few programs for your computer area, which should you buy? To answer this frequently asked question, we've compiled a preschool "starter set" for Apple, for Commodore, and for IBM. These three sets are listed in Table 2. (Note that each program's producer is indicated in parentheses in the table. Complete names and addresses of producers mentioned in this book are given in the Appendix.) Because these starter sets of programs may provide a child's first experience with computer activities, we chose **easy-to-use** programs, ones that assure a successful and rewarding first experience. We also tried to compose each set so that it **covers an adequate range of learning experiences**.

Table 3 lists starter sets for kindergarten. All the programs in the starter sets have simple menus that make activity selection easy for children right from the start. They're all appropriate for most kindergarten children and provide a range of challenges to accommodate less-mature as well as more-advanced children.

As you become comfortable with computers in the classroom, you may want more varied or specific computer activities for certain areas of the curriculum. There are many other good programs, and new ones are being published regularly. In the chapters

Table 2

Preschool Starter Programs

Main Focus	Program Title	A Starter[a] for Apple II	IBM	C64	Program Description
Language	*Muppets On Stage* (Sunburst)	•	•	•	Introduces letters, numbers, and colors with animation, sound. Has options for selecting letters and numbers to suit child.
Language	*Kid's Stuff* (Stone)		•		Children match letter outlines with keys to spell out words, whose referents are then shown in colorful animation.
Number	*Number Farm* (DLM)	•	•	•	Six games introduce counting, estimating, and numeral recognition.
Classification	*Observation and Classification* (Hartley)	•			Involves judgments of similarity, difference, and inclusion in category. Four games with three levels of challenge.
Classification	*Kindercomp* (Spinnaker)			•	Clever matching activity involving shapes, colors, and directional discrimination.
Classification	*Kindercomp Golden Edition* (Spinnaker)		•		One of its eight activities is a good matching activity. Also has alphabet, letter recognition, number activities.
Ordering	*Size and Logic* (Hartley)	•			Provides exercises in size discrimination and in duplicating or extending pattern sequences.
Time/Spatial relations	*Estimation* (Lawrence)	•			Children gauge times, speed, and distance in stopping a train.
Spatial relations	*Ernie's Big Splash* (Hi Tech)			•	Children use directional skills to create waterways so that a rubber duck can reach a Muppet character. **Requires joystick**.
Creative activity	*Color Me* (Mindscape)	•	•	•	Allows children to create and print computer art involving lines and color and to write accompanying text. **Requires mouse or joystick, and printer**.
Creative activity	*Mask Parade* (Springboard)	•	•	•	Children create and print masks or accessories that they can color and wear and incorporate in role play. **Requires printer**.

[a]A suggested "starter program" for a given brand of computer may also be available for other computers. This table suggests the *strongest* starter program available in a particular subject area for each computer brand.

Table 3

Kindergarten Starter Programs

Main Focus	Program Title	A Starter[a] for			Program Description
		Apple II	**IBM**	**C64**	
Language	*Fun From A to Z* (MECC)	•			Introduces letters and alphabetical order through letter-matching, dot-to-dot, and other activities. Teacher can pace and vary level of challenge.
Language	*Stickybear Reading* (Weekly Reader)			•	Children can discover word meanings and word order when phrases are animated after child selects words.
Language	*Easy as ABC* (Springboard)		•		Five activities give practice with letter recognition and alphabetical order.
Number	*Counting Critters* (MECC)	•			Children match numerals; count sets of objects, selected objects within a set. Teacher can select numbers used.
Number	*Number Farm* (DLM)			•	Six games introduce counting, estimating, numeral recognition.
Number	*Math Rabbit* (Learning Co.)		•		Introduces counting and comparing sets (greater than, less than). Provides beginning addition, subtraction activities.
Classification	*Gertrude's Secrets* (Learning Co.)	•	•	•	Children solve problems involving similarities, differences.
Ordering	*Patterns and Sequences* (Hartley)	•			Children match shape and color patterns in four activities, each with three levels of challenge.
Spatial relations	*Stickybear Town Builder* (Weekly Reader)	•	•	•	Develops directional concepts as children navigate around a town. **Joystick recommended**.
Time/Spatial relations	*Estimation* (Lawrence)	•			Children gauge time, speed, and distance in stopping a train.
Creative activity	*Color Me* (Mindscape)	•	•	•	Allows children to create and print computer art involving lines and color and to write accompanying text. **Requires mouse or joystick, and printer**.

[a]A suggested "starter program" for a given brand of computer may also be available for other computers. This table suggests the *strongest* starter program available in a particular subject area for each computer brand.

that follow, we describe additional programs and how they might fit into specific areas of the early childhood curriculum.

How Much Will It All Cost?

The basic equipment and software described in this chapter can be put together in various ways, depending on the brands you select, the peripherals you decide you need, and the number of programs you buy to get started. To get an idea of the total outlay required, we might compute **the cost of a hypothetical "package" composed of ten starter programs and a computer with disk drive, a color monitor, and two peripherals—a printer and a mouse**. If we suppose that the ten starter programs will cost an average of $30 apiece, **this package would cost you $1,250–$2,200**. If you choose a Laser 128, Commodore 64, or IBM-compatible computer, the price of your system will be at the lower end of this price range; if you choose an Apple or IBM computer, the price will be at the upper end of this price range. Deciding to begin with **three computers, instead of only one, but all the same equipment and software just described, would cost $2,750–$5,000**.

Summary

By now, you should have a grasp of how to select computer equipment for use with young children. Minimal requirements are a computer, disk drive, and color monitor. Standard models of Apple or Apple compatibles, Commodore, and IBM or its compatibles have available a sufficient variety of appropriate software for use in early childhood classrooms. **Because good-quality software is the key to young children's computer learning, you should have a good idea of the suitability of specific equipment to desired software before you select computer equipment.**

While hardware selection involves careful consideration both of short- and long-term consequences, it is a decision that, once made, quickly takes a back seat to the question of how to use computers to help children learn. This is the topic we turn to in the chapters that follow.

3 Using Computers Throughout the Day

The following scenario is based on observations from a real preschool classroom. If reading it makes you feel uncomfortable, this may be because it highlights common traps we are all likely to fall into when we introduce children to computers.

It's the beginning of the day at the preschool, and the teacher and aide are talking with the children, helping them plan their morning activities. The classroom is divided into several well-equipped activity areas, including a computer area. The area has one computer, which is ready to load the Stickybear Numbers program (by Weekly Reader).

"The computer area will be open today at work time," the teacher says. "You can use the computer yourself, but I or Mrs. G. must help you."

Mrs. G. asks, "How long can we stay at the computer?"

"Four minutes," says the teacher. Since she wants each child to have a turn at the computer, she limits the time for any one child. She also intends that children will come to the computer area one at a time—a pattern she has introduced in earlier work times.

Work time begins. Alex is the first to come to the computer. Mrs. G. is there and is starting up Stickybear Numbers. She tells Alex to use the spacebar or the number keys but not the other keys.

Alex pushes the spacebar, but nothing happens (the program is still loading). "Don't push the keys when the red light is on," says Mrs. G., pointing to the disk drive's operating light. After this, Alex intently watches the disk drive light but doesn't pay much attention to the screen as he presses the spacebar.

Alex's time at the computer is up, and Toni takes his place. Mrs. G. reviews the rules for Toni: "Watch the red light, don't touch any keys if the red light is on, and touch only the number keys and the spacebar."

She adds, "I'm going to have to ask you to leave the computer if you touch anything but the number keys or spacebar."

After only a short time at the computer, Toni decides on her own to leave the computer because she is concerned that she might do something to displease Mrs. G.

It's Warren's turn now. Warren remembers the rules and alternates between the spacebar

and the number keys. He likes the spacebar because it makes the screen display change so quickly—and it produces an additional banana each time he presses it! Pressing the number keys, he has found, changes the display more slowly.

"What kind of fruit are these?" asks Mrs. G. "Let's count them." Warren points to some of the bananas on the screen as he counts. "No, let's try counting

this way, instead," says Mrs. G. Moving from left to right, she points out each banana while Warren counts. "Just the number keys," she reminds Warren.

Warren is now really absorbed, counting the objects on the screen and pushing the number keys in response. But his time is up, and he must leave to make room for the next child.

Before commenting on the negative aspects of the scenario, let's consider what's right about the classroom it portrays: The classroom is nicely arranged into a variety of inviting activity areas, each well stocked with an array of materials. Children spend time with adults, planning which areas they will visit and what they will do there. Activities in the areas are varied and creative. The adults have created learning opportunities that are in tune with children's needs and interests. In addition, the classroom is fortunate enough to have a computer that children can use on their own.

However, computers are new to the classroom, and these adults are not quite sure they have found the most effective way to integrate them into the learning environment. They've made a concerted effort to make the computer area inviting for children, but they're not ready to let children explore the area on their own. Overprotectiveness—toward the children and toward the machine—is evident in Mrs. G.'s behavior. She lets children know there

is just one right way to use the computer. Mrs. G. is quite diligent in making sure the children use the computer "correctly," but she is sensing that her diligence is stultifying children's exploration and discovery. What can Mrs. G. do to rectify this situation? We would offer the following suggestions:

■ **Understand and care for your computer, but don't overcomplicate children's use of the machine with unnecessary warnings about care and handling.** Microcomputers are surprisingly robust machines. They can break, of course, but they are designed for heavy use. Good software for children allows all kinds of keys to be struck without causing the computer to jam or lose its place. Mrs. G.'s concern over the disk drive light is unnecessary. Children will find out through experience that there are moments when the computer is unre-

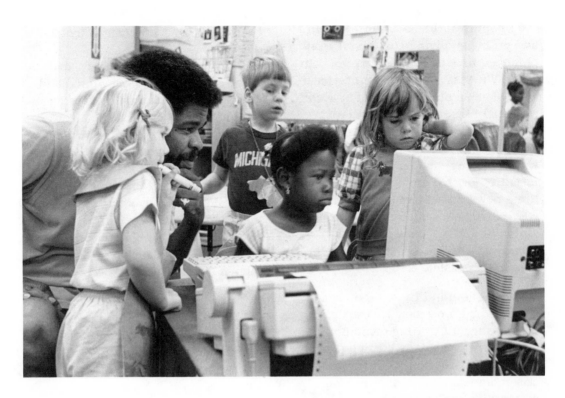

Teachers can encourage the problem solving that results from children working together at the computer.

sponsive. They will learn to wait a moment and try again. No damage can be done to the computer by typing when the disk drive is operating.

■ **Introduce programs to all children in teacher-led group sessions; then encourage children to work at the computer on their own.** As noted throughout this book, young children need some adult help to make computer programs work successfully. Introductory activities are usually necessary to illustrate the operation of a particular computer activity and to highlight the concepts and skills involved. After introducing the program, however, you can let children master it on their own. If the software is developmentally appropriate, children will soon learn how to operate the program.

Good computer activities, by allowing many "right" ways to lead to desired results, permit children to solve problems in their own way. The computer activity isn't doing its job if children can't use it without constant prompting from an adult.

■ **Allow each child's attention-span and interest-level to regulate independent use of the computer.** Setting a time-limit on young children's computer use usually isn't necessary, since in a well-designed early childhood classroom, the computer area is only one among several attractive areas that children may choose to work in. Also, any given computer activity will appeal to some children more than to others, so the amount of time that different children spend at a computer will vary.

■ **Encourage the social interaction and problem solving that result from children working together at the computer.** Whereas some children prefer to work alone, a strict one-child-at-a-time rule might discourage an insecure child from trying the computer activity. Being able to work at the computer with a partner might be just the right incentive for that child to try something new and achieve much-needed success. Also, for such a child, explanation or advice from a friend or friends can be less intimidating than an adult's assistance.

Keeping in mind these broad suggestions, let's now look at specific methods for integrating computer learning with the daily life of an early childhood classroom. Whether your classroom is a preschool or kindergarten, this daily life probably includes a time schedule that is more or less consistent, and any computer activities you choose must fit into this schedule—along with other learning activities, with large- and small-group times, with snack and rest times, with clean-up and outdoor times. The remainder of this chapter will suggest ways to work the computer in among all this; it will also suggest ways that the computer can work into, and perhaps shorten, your schedule of classroom administrative tasks.

In our classroom, computers fit most easily into small- and large-group times and into the children's independent work time. The key to successful computer activity seems to be to introduce each new program in a group activity, which is a strategy we discuss in the following section, along with other ways to use the computer in group activities.

Computers at Group Time

In the High/Scope classroom, small-group time is a teacher-planned and teacher-led activity that focuses on introducing a material (such as play dough or a tape recorder) or a concept (such as ordering objects by size, or counting objects) in a way that incorporates children's ideas. It is therefore an ideal time to introduce a new computer program that ties in with some concept that is being developed.

We made the following general observations from our experience using the computer in small-group activities:

■ Most computer programs are best introduced with a hands-on preliminary activity involving objects such as blocks, beads, counters, drawing materials.

■ After a computer activity has been introduced at small-group time, it often becomes a popular choice with children during the times they work independently, giving them more experience with the skill or concept developed in the small group.

■ In grasping a new concept, some children respond better to the impersonal feedback of a computer than to the feedback of a teacher.

■ Using an appropriate, ready-made computer activity to introduce or elaborate on a concept at small-group time can reduce a teacher's preparation time.

We also drew some more specific conclusions about what works best when using the computer in group times, as you will see from the sections that follow.

Conducting the Group Time

In our classroom, one of the three computers in the computer area is on a cart with wheels, which makes it easy to bring the computer to another part of the room for a small-group activity. An extension cord attached to the cart permits us to plug in the computer wherever it is moved.

For small-group time, the computer cart is rolled up next to the teacher's chair. This gives the teacher a view of the screen and also allows the children, if they are seated in a circle with the teacher, to focus attention on both the computer and the teacher. After a preliminary activity with concrete materials illustrating the concept or skill featured in the computer program (box, p. 42), the teacher turns the monitor on. (This is assuming the teacher has started up the computer ahead of time, so the program is already at the section the teacher wishes to use.)

With the computer activity on the screen, the teacher can ask questions that solicit responses from the children for each step of the activity: "How can we make the arrow move?" "What does this key do?" A teacher can enter responses, or better still, ask children to take turns at the keyboard. Since many of the child responses in programs for this age group involve using just a few keys, having children take turns at the keyboard is not time-consuming. Using a computer with a small or detachable keyboard (detachables like the Apple IIGS or the IBM and

During a small-group introduction of a computer activity, the teacher can stop and discuss a question, picture, or response at any time.

compatibles, or computers small enough to pass around, like the Commodore 64 and the Apple IIc) makes it possible to pass the keyboard around the table while the monitor stays on the cart. This enables children to take turns more quickly and easily. (Alternative input devices, such as the joystick or mouse, also lend themselves to taking turns in this way.)

The teacher can stop and discuss a question, picture, or response at any time during the computer program or may interrupt the computer work to introduce some related activity with concrete materials. While some children are taking turns at the computer, others will choose to continue working with concrete materials. When most children seem comfortable with using the computer program, the teacher can announce when it will be available for them to use independently in the computer area.

Small-group activities carried out in this way throughout the year have successfully eased computer learning into our High/Scope classroom.

A Preliminary Activity for Stickybear Town Builder

S*tickybear Town Builder* (Weekly Reader) is a computer program in which young children create a town map and then practice their direction skills by guiding a car to specific destinations. The following town-building activity can help older preschoolers and kindergarters get the most out of the *Stickybear* program. The activity requires these materials:

■ A large sheet of paper that covers the table, with some simple roads drawn on it

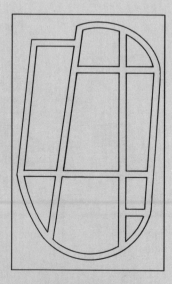

■ A colored marker for each child

■ Match-box-sized cars, one for each child

One way to begin is by telling the children that you would like them to help create a toy town by drawing buildings on the paper. You can ask them what kinds of buildings they're drawing (fire department, supermarket, library), to familiarize everyone with the names and locations of the buildings being drawn.

After some buildings are drawn, you might introduce the cars by driving a car to each child. The children will enjoy driving their cars around the roads, from building to building. Next, turn to the computer monitor (with *Stickybear*

Town Builder loaded in the computer) and explain to the children that you are going to help them get started on a computer activity in which they can practice driving from one building to another. Use one of the program's built-in towns, or use a town you might have built and saved at an earlier time. While children are drawing or driving their cars around the large paper map, encourage interested children to drive the computer car to destinations in the *Stickybear* town.

When each interested child has had an opportunity to drive to one of the on-screen destinations, explain that the *Stickybear* program will be available for them to use on their own in the computer area at work time.

Frequency of Computer-Based Group Times

How frequently should computer small-group times occur for preschool and kindergarten children? We find that a small-group computer time about once a week works well. Since a given computer program may contain multiple activities, several successive small-group times may be devoted to the activities in one program. At the beginning of the year, teachers make a general plan indicating the programs to be used that year. Throughout the year, they adjust and add detail to this plan to accommodate the skills and interests of the children and to coordinate computer activities with other classroom activities.

The lists in Tables 2 and 3 of the previous chapter describe the content areas of recommended starter programs, to help teachers in their general planning for use of the programs. The earlier-mentioned *High/Scope Survey of Early Childhood Software* also contains lists categorizing its programs according to content.

Using a Large-Group Introduction

The techniques just outlined for small-group introduction of a computer activity might, particularly in classrooms with just one adult, be applied to large-group or circle time. In a large group, of course, there is less opportunity for individuals to be actively involved with the computer. Despite such limitations, such introductory activities are essential to prepare children for successful independent work at computers and should be planned even for larger groups when necessary.

Occasionally a teacher may find a computer program that does not require a detailed introduction, perhaps because children have had some experience with similar computer activities. In such a case, as children gather at the welcome circle, the teacher might briefly introduce and demonstrate the new program, letting several children try it out. After this brief introduction, the program can be placed in the computer area for children to use independently.

Before work time, a child writes out his plan for an activity in the computer area.

Computers at Work Time

In the daily routine of the High/Scope classroom, after a preliminary planning time when children and adults meet together and talk about each child's activity plan, children have a work time to carry out their individual plans. Many preschool and kindergarten classes follow a similar procedure, allowing children to choose to work in one or more areas around the room—in the art area, block area, house area, or quiet area, for example. In the High/Scope demonstration classroom, spending work time in the computer area with a previously introduced computer activity is one of the many choices available to children. They may choose to work singly or with one or more partners, and since there are multiple computers, they have a choice of programs.

Some days, especially just after the introduction of a new program, too many children choose the computer area. This presents an appropriate problem for young children to solve. One way they might choose to handle

this situation is by drawing names to decide which of them will work in the computer area that day; sometimes a second drawing, from the remaining names, may be necessary to determine who will work in the computer area the following day. Valuable lessons about problem solving, fair play, and planning ahead can result.

During children's independent use of the computer, adults are available to assist children as needed and to talk with them about their work. Adults may use this time, for example, to point out keys the program uses frequently (if the children do not already know them) or to ask the children to describe their work so far and what they plan to do next. We recommend using open-ended questions (such as "What do you think will happen if. . .") as much as possible, to elicit the children's own thinking. Again, teachers who avoid the overprotective and overly directive behaviors illustrated in the scenario that opens this chapter allow

During children's independent use of the computer, adults are available to assist children as needed and to talk with them about their work.

It is not uncommon for one or more children to develop a particular expertise with the computer and to offer "technical assistance" to others.

children to become truly engaged in their work at the computer.

To facilitate very young children's work in the computer area, it is helpful to insert the program disks in the computer and start up the computer at the beginning of the day. Once the pro-gram is loaded into the computer, the monitor can then be turned off until work time. This not only heads off difficulty children might have locating the proper disk and inserting it into the computer, it also avoids making them wait while the program loads.

For children who seem interested and ready, to further enhance their independence and ability to make choices, you can introduce inserting disks and loading the program into the computer. An alternative to having *every* child handle the disks is to appoint a responsible computer helper, on a rotating basis, to load the disks and start the computer each day and to turn off the computer at the end of the day. Remember, however, that the more hands you involve in disk use, the greater the chances of disk damage. Disks are likely to keep working for many years, but as we mentioned in Chapter 2, it is prudent to take some care in handling them and to have back-up copies to keep your computer center functioning should a disk fail.

Before leaving the topic of children's independent computer use, lest we give the impression that teachers must constantly hover over the computer area, we want to emphasize the trouble-shooting role that preschoolers and kindergartners play for one another at work time in the computer center. Because children delight so in the success they experience after mastering a computer activity, they are often anxious to share their knowledge with other children in the classroom. It is not uncommon for one or more children to develop a particular expertise with the computer and to offer "technical assistance" to others experiencing some difficulty. In the High/Scope classroom, adults support this tendency by encouraging children to ask one another for help. This way, a

Observations at Work Time

How much time do preschool children spend at computers? How much of this time is spent productively? To answer these and related questions about young children's computer use, we conducted an informal study over a two-week period at the High/Scope demonstration classroom. A total of 14 three- to five-year-old children of varied socioeconomic and ethnic backgrounds participated in the study; the average

classroom attendance during our observations was just over 10 children per day.

The daily 50 minutes of work time, during which children choose to work at one or more of the classroom's activity areas, was the time we used for observing which children selected the computer area, what they did there, and how much time they spent there. Here's what we found over five work-time observations:

■ In 21 of 29 child visits to the computer area, children spent time using the computers in a substantive way, rather than simply stopping in the area or watching classmates use the computers.

■ These substantive computer encounters lasted an average of 12 minutes each, and two encounters lasted more than 20 minutes.

■ In the 8 computer encounters that we didn't

consider substantive, children pushed a few keys and left, used the computer without really understanding what they were doing, or simply stayed in the computer area to watch what was going on. Nevertheless, all but one of the children involved in these less-productive encounters had productive experiences at least one other time during our observations. Thus it appears that children who watch other children at the computers or just stop to press a few buttons may actually be learning something useful (see One Child's Mastery of *Color Me* in Chapter 6).

■ The nearly 12 minutes children averaged at the computers was sufficient for them to play a whole game, complete a drawing, or work through several parts of an activity. This average of 12 minutes per computer encounter means that a classroom with one computer can provide each child with several productive computer sessions per week, especially if children work in pairs. Furthermore, 12 minutes of computer activity several times a week leaves each child with ample time to engage in other classroom activities.

■ Ten of the 14 children observed had at least one session of "quality time" with the computers.

■ Most of the children observed were able to make good use of the computer and to do so without adult help; the teacher's introduction to the computer activities during previous small-group sessions was apparently ample preparation for independent work.

It appears that children who simply watch other children at the computers may also be learning something useful.

child with a problem gains a non-threatening helper, the helper builds his or her sense of competence and self-esteem, and both children gain a potential friend.

Besides being well suited to independent work time, the computer can also aid in some whole-group tasks that are common in the early childhood classroom. These group tasks are often relegated to circle time, which we discuss next.

Computers at Circle Time

Writing group stories is one circle-time activity to which a computer contributes immensely, especially when it comes to editing or revising and to printing multiple copies of the story. Group stories may relate the experiences of a field trip, or they may be creative stories around such themes as a holiday or "our families." (We'll talk more about this in Chapter 4 when discussing word-processing programs.)

Circle time in many preschools and kindergartens is also the time when children share experiences with one another by showing something they have made or something they have brought from home and telling other children about it. The computer printout from a child's earlier drawing or writing activity—or one or two screen dump pictures from any computer activity the child has recently enjoyed—can be objects for this "show and tell" activity.

If a child has a computer picture to share, the teacher might help by adding one-word, written labels to important parts of the picture as the child talks about it with the group. The teacher, by asking what colors the child plans to use for different parts of

the picture, could also encourage the child to extend the activity.

By showing the products of their computer work and talking about what they did to create them and what their future plans are, children can develop a valuable awareness of their own actions and ideas; they can see the relationship between what they plan to do and what they accomplish. (This recalling, or summing up, of work-time activities is such a significant part of the High/Scope classroom's curriculum that a special time is set apart for it, in small groups, immediately following work and clean-up.)

If young children are encouraged to share computer experiences in this way, their computer learning will not fit the stereotypical view of computer activities as promoting children's isolation and self-absorption. The computer will be used not as an end in itself but as one of many tools for experiencing and for representing one's experiences.

Now that you have seen how the classroom's daily schedule—in particular how small-group time, work time, recall time, and circle time—can make room for computer learning, consider how that computer in your classroom might also work its way into *your* schedule by simplifying and shortening some of your administrative and supportive tasks.

Computers for Teacher Tasks

So far we've talked a lot about the many ways we have seen computers help young children learn, but our experience has also shown ways that early childhood educators themselves can benefit from the availability of a computer. The same computers the children are using can lighten your

By showing the printed products of their computer work to others, children can develop pride in the tangible results of their own ideas and actions.

workload if you know about the following opportunities for computer use:

Writing Letters, Reports, Plans

Writing on the computer can be much easier and less frustrating than writing at a typewriter. Errors are easy to correct, editing and revision are easy, and results can be saved and reused with minor adaptations at another time. So consider using your classroom computer for writing letters to parents, children's progress reports, and even lesson plans. For these purposes, you'll need a word-processing program, and if you are inhibited by the keyboard, there are even computer programs to help you improve your typing (see box, p. 52, for suggested programs). However, it's good to know that *perfect* typing skill is even less important on the computer than on the typewriter, because of the ease of making corrections.

Making Signs and Posters

There are poster-making programs you can use with your computer to make posters for notices of parent meetings, rummage sales, children's programs, and class presentations. Poster making requires minimal typing, since the letters are large and only a few words are required. In addition, poster-making programs usually provide pictures that can be included on the poster to help get your message across. Several programs can also be used to make labels and signs for the classroom (box, p. 52). For example, to promote children's independent use of materials and areas, you can add word labels to pictures depicting crayons, scissors, and paste in the art area or you can make signs for the sink, refrigerator, and stove in the house area.

Keeping Classroom Records

Maintaining classroom records can drain a good deal of a teacher's energy. While computers will not eliminate paperwork, they can make it easier for you to keep up with it, once you've cleared the initial hurdles of computerizing records. For example, class rosters with names, addresses, parents' names, emergency numbers, immunization dates, and other vital information can be readily organized with a record-keeping program called a database program (box, p. 55). What's nice about computers doing the work is that records for new children and new categories of information can be added easily without having to make the record forms over again. A revised report can be printed each time any item is added or changed. The computer's capacity to quickly retrieve and sort information for easy comparisons (for example, reviewing all the children's progress in a particular curriculum area) is another advantage of computerized record keeping.

Records of children's progress, such as daily notes on children's activities and social development, are tedious and time-consuming to keep by hand. But keeping some record of a child's daily experience is important in the short run for planning new experiences for the child and in the long run for reporting progress to parents and to succeeding teachers. A computer can ease the task of note taking and help with sorting out the information that accumulates.

You can make posters or notices for parent meetings, rummage sales, children's programs, and class presentations with computer programs like The Printshop.

Programs for Teacher Use

■ **For your writing:** Among word-processing programs for Apple II computers (and compatibles), *Magic Slate* (Sunburst), *The Bank Street Writer III* (Scholastic), and *AppleWorks* (CLARIS) stand out for their ease of use and flexibility. All three provide a full range of word-processing features, such as moving sections of text, deleting, underlining, boldfacing, and centering. Both *Magic Slate* and *The Bank Street Writer III* can display standard-sized letters as well as large letters suitable for children's stories and dictation.

For the Commodore 64, *Geos WRITER 64* (Berkeley) and *The Bank Street Writer* (Broderbund), are two easy-to-use word-processing programs suited for teachers' correspondence and other typing needs.

For IBM and compatible computers, a whole host of word-processing programs are available, including many full-featured packages designed to satisfy the needs of professional writers and editors. Among the low-cost and easy-to-use ones are *The Bank Street Writer* and *Easy Working: The Writer* (Spinnaker).

■ **For your typing skills:** To learn or brush up on touch-typing, consider using *Typing Tutor IV* (Simon & Schuster), which is available for all three machines.

■ **For your signs, posters, and labels:** The poster-making program that has put computer-generated signs, banners, and notices on innumerable school, business, and church bulletin boards is *The Print Shop* (Broderbund). Though many alternatives exist, this classic program will most likely meet your sign- and poster-making needs and is available for nearly every computer model. *The Print Shop*, which uses only upper-case letters, can also be used to make classroom labels.

You might also consider using one of the following computer programs to make classroom labels and signs:

1. *Magic Slate* (Sunburst), *The Bank Street Writer III*—Word-processing programs with large, 20-column letters, both upper- and lower-case. These letters are only about ½ × ¼ inch, not as large as those produced by *The Print Shop*.

2. *MacWrite* (CLARIS)—Produces labels with even larger letters than the above programs offer, but requires access to an Apple Macintosh computer. This word-processing program produces labels of various sizes in both upper- and lower-case letters.

Across the top of a typical High/Scope classroom observation chart, nine major program goal areas are listed: language, representation, classification, and so on. Below these headings are blank columns where important events in the child's learning can be described briefly. High/Scope teachers find it easiest to keep a page of these records for each child in the class. If you use this system, you don't need to enter notes on each child every day; rather, you can highlight a few children in each day's notes.

Over the span of several weeks, this system can provide cumulative information about each child's progress in various curriculum areas. By glancing at the pages, the teacher can tell which children have not been observed recently and which areas of the curriculum need more focus in the days and weeks to come.

These records are easy to computerize. Keeping track of them on the computer has several advantages—as well as a few disadvantages. One major advantage in using the computer is that the records are all typed and easy to read. In addition, the computer can

A typical High/Scope classroom observation form, with a teacher's notes on a child

Child Assessment Record (C.A.R.)
© 1987 High/Scope Educational Research Foundation

Child's Name: Jason   *Remember to date all entries.*

LANGUAGE	REPRESENTATION	CLASSIFICATION	SERIATION	NUMBER	SPACE	TIME	MOVEMENT	SOC/EMOTIONAL
7/10 Cut playdough into pieces and labeled it "pizza."	7/26 Followed motions for Skinna Ma Rink song.	7/8 Told Ann to hang her sign in the art area when working. 7/28 Told us fancy rabbit was made by scissors		7/9 Brought 4 blocks, did 1-1 correspondence up to 4. 7/17 counted 1-1 up to 6 including self.	7/10 Successfully used joystick to play "Ducks Ahoy." 7/29 Circled area on planning sheet.	7/10 After being shown once, did "Ducks Ahoy" on own. 7/17 Reminded Ann to put away toys before making new plan.		7/9 Stayed close to teacher before beginning to play.

Name	Date	Lang	Rep	Class	Ser	Numb	Space	Time	Move	SocEm	Comments
Jason	Jul 8			X							Told Ann to hang her sign in art area when working
Jason	Jul 9									X	Stayed close to teacher before beginning to play
Jason	Jul 9				X						Brought 4 blocks, did 1-1 correspondance up to 4
Jason	Jul 10	X									Cut play dough into pieces and labeled it "pizza."
Jason	Jul 10						X				Succesfully used joystick to play "Ducks Ahoy"
Jason	Jul 10							X			After being shown once did "Ducks Ahoy" on own
Jason	Jul 17				X						Counted 1-1 up to 6 including self
Jason	Jul 17							X			Reminded Ann to put away toys before making new plan.
Jason	Jul 26		X								Followed motions for Skinna Ma Rink song
Jason	Jul 28			X							Told us fancy rabbit was made by the scissors.
Jason	Jul 29						X				Circled area on planning sheet

A computer version of the same observation notes

sort records in any order, so records can be sorted and displayed according to a specific need: by day, by groups of children, or by curriculum topic, for example. Periodic reports can then be printed, perhaps to review the activities a particular child has engaged in or to indicate which children have gone unobserved for significant periods of time.

These printouts of computerized records can also be a great help when preparing for meetings with parents or when sending a progress report home. The teacher simply calls up the records of a given child and prints them out or summarizes them in a letter for parents. The computerized record system also comes in handy when making mid-year or year-end assessments of a child, since all the records are readily available for printing and review.

A minor disadvantage of a computerized record-keeping system— besides the fact that it requires typing ability— is that you can't see more than one screen of information at a time. If you are used to spreading pages in front of you and scanning them, it takes a while to get used to working with screens of information and moving back and forth from one to another. It helps to print out the information periodically to get the overall picture. Such printouts also provide a way of keeping records current, even on days when the computer is not available or, for some reason, not working. In these cases, information can be penciled in, to be typed into the computer at another time. Another important reminder: When using a computerized record-keeping system, be sure to make a back-up copy of your files, just in case something should happen to your working copies.

More Programs for Teacher Use

■ **For your record keeping:** *AppleWorks* (CLARIS) for Apple II (and compatibles), in addition to providing word processing, includes an easy-to-use database program that will meet most if not all of the record-keeping needs of early childhood educators. The database portion of the program uses many of the same keys as the word-processing part, so learning one helps you with the other. For Commodore and IBM computers respectively, such easy-to-use database programs as *Geos FILER 64* (Berkeley) and *Easy Working: The Filer* (Spinnaker) are good places to start with classroom record keeping.

■ **For your budgets:** The *AppleWorks* program for Apple II (and compatible) computers also contains a spreadsheet program, and it is as easy to use as the word-processing and database portions of the *AppleWorks* program. For Commodore and IBM (and compatible) computers respectively, *Geos Swift-CALC 64* (Berkeley) and *Easy Working: The Planner* (Spinnaker) are inexpensive and easy-to-use spreadsheet programs.

Preparing Budgets

If you've ever been faced with budgeting a limited amount of money for a variety of classroom supplies, you know it can be a chore to get it all to add up as planned. Using a computer with a simple accounting, or "spreadsheet," program (see box) can make this kind of budgeting much easier. And you'll never make a mistake with the arithmetic, since the computer does it for you.

Telecomputing

Many teachers turn to journals, newsletters, and conferences for fresh ideas that help them develop professionally. A computer with a phone hookup allows access to a variety of information sources of potential interest to teachers. These include special-interest "bulletin boards" and national information services like Compuserve or DIALOG. The latter both provide a number of services of specific interest to teachers, including bibliographic services such as indexes of microcomputer journals and the ERIC database of educational publications.

While it is not necessary to understand word processing, databases, or telecomputing to effectively use computers in teaching, these can be valuable personal skills for any adult, and those who gain these skills will be more comfortable and confident in using computers with children and in working with parents who are knowledgeable about computers.

*In a High/Scope computer
training workshop, adults
have access to knowledge-
able instructors and a
chance to freely explore the
computer programs.*

Finding Time for Computers

By now you may realize ways the computer can be timesaving and also time-consuming. Incorporating computer programs into the daily routine is much like incorporating any other classroom tool: Children need an initial introduction to their use and some teacher support while using them, but much of children's work with computers is also done independently. In this respect, then, the computer is no more or less demanding of teacher time than other classroom equipment or materials are. Furthermore, once teachers are familiar with using the computer for such tasks as writing reports, budgeting, and sign or label making, it can actually save some valuable teacher time.

The largest demand on teacher time and energy occurs initially, when the computer equipment and programs are new, and adults in the classroom must familiarize themselves all at once with the system and the starter programs. We recommend doing this in a training workshop outside of regular classroom hours. In this way, an extended period is available for a knowledgeable instructor to demonstrate computer learning activities and, most important, for teachers to freely explore the computer programs.

Summary

In this chapter, we have described roles that computers play for both children and adults in the typical preschool and kindergarten day. Computer use is not limited to a fixed "computer time" but can make important contributions throughout the day, fitting in with young children's varied interests and abilities and providing them with choices and chances to initiate their own activities. In the next chapter, we look at the specific ways classroom computers can assist in young children's development of language skills.

④ Computers and Young Children's Language Development

Concern by parents, teachers, public institutions, and private businesses for a literate public creates a favorable climate for developing and marketing language-oriented computer programs. Consequently, almost half the existing programs for young children deal with emerging reading and writing skills. In this chapter, we look in some detail at this application of computers to children's early language development.

The computer is well suited to the task of handling language. (In fact, although the computer's ability to perform long or complex numerical computations caused its early success, it is now its ability to handle words and word processing that makes it popular in many settings.) Computers can display words and letters on the screen and allow them to be moved about at will; the computer's graphic capabilities can produce pictures and other related images—some with actions and movements—to accompany the words and letters; and printers allow screen words and pictures to be transferred to paper. More recently, special computer attachments enable

computers to speak, to read from books, and to a limited extent, to understand spoken words. No wonder computers are being harnessed to help children learn about language!

But the application of computers to preschoolers' and kindergartners' language learning raises some questions: Can the computer be a channel through which a young child's development and learning flow naturally together? Is the computer a tool that can help children convert their spoken language skills into literacy and creative expression? Or is the computer the ultimate weapon for those who would push academic learning further downward into early childhood? To answer these questions, we first look at the language skills, interests, and tendencies children already have between the ages of three and six. Then we examine how existing computer programs can support and develop these.

Reading and Writing—What Precedes It?

Early childhood researchers use the term **emergent literacy** to describe the early stages children go through on their way to developing conventional reading and writing skills. Those who have studied children's emergent literacy report that children, even at a very early age, demonstrate a surprising amount of savvy about and interest in the written word.

Children only around two years old, for example, will sometimes "read" a book, although this "reading" is usually not word-for-word decoding but a spoken labeling of pictures as they turn the pages of a book. Gradually, the emerging reader uses longer and longer phrases, and even sentences, in conjunction with the pictures. These very young children often have their own taste in literature—preferring to read a favorite book over and over even though other familiar books are available.

Preschool children often identify print as "writing" or "words" and commonly ask adults to read words to them from signs, labels, and books—"What does this say?" or "Read this" are familiar refrains to parents and other caregivers. Three- and four-year-olds like to pretend to read, imitating the posture and speech of adults who have read to them. They also realize there is a difference between story-style speech and conversation-style speech: When telling a story, they often include such stylistic features as a setting (Once upon a time. . .), direct quotation (The witch said. . .), and a

conclusion (They all lived happily ever after)—all of which are absent when the same children talk about daily events. When they are telling a "book" story, their voices may also become deeper and fuller, as if they were speaking to an audience.

Three- and four-year-olds also possess considerable knowledge about writing. They often scribble something or write one or two letters for "words" and frequently express themselves in pictures that tell a story. They eagerly learn to identify their own written names, and they watch with interest when an adult writes. Dictating a story so an adult can write it down is enjoyable to them; children dictating have been known to slow their speech and emphasize breaks between words, which would indicate their recognition of the writer's task of recording one word at a time.

Emergent literacy in kindergartners begins to resemble more closely the conventional skills of reading and writing. Around age five, children see similarities and differences that enable them to match, or recognize, letters. They want to write their own names. Using contextual clues or clues of shape, they begin to recognize words other than their own names. They will attempt to "read" familiar storybooks and transcripts of their own dictation (relying mostly on memory and contextual clues).

More advanced kindergartners are interested in identifying all the letters of the alphabet and might even enjoy reciting them in alphabetical order (though this doesn't indicate an ability to alphabetize or recognize where a specific letter fits into the alphabet). These children may begin to associate sounds with letters, even to recognize initial consonants in words. Their word awareness increases as well. They can match printed words that are the same and words that rhyme; they begin to note the same letter combinations in different words (for example, the "ank" in "bank" and "tank"); and they can see shorter words inside of longer words (like the "at" in "mat"). With this increased word awareness comes the desire and ability to write several words other than their own names. They may devise their own spellings for words.

Researchers, such as Elizabeth Sulzby and W. H. Teale, believe that by recognizing these emerging skills, interests, and tendencies in young children, adults can help them to explore written language and to build on knowledge they already possess, well before the children have mastered all the component reading and writing skills of phonics, spelling, grammar, and printing (see *Emergent Literacy: Writing and Reading*, Ablex, 1986). Thus, children will approach written language in much the same way that they approach spoken language, by acquiring a facility with it before attending to its finer details. This early encouragement and support, according to the researchers, can facilitate later attainment of the conventional reading and writing skills.

Of course, one way to support this emergent literacy is to do what many parents and other caregivers have been doing all along—reading to their preschoolers and kindergartners, modeling writing for them, taking their dictation, showing interest in their attempts at reading and writing, and supplying them with books, pencils, crayons, markers, and stacks of paper. Modern technology makes it possible to supply children with another literacy tool—the computer.

From the description of emergent literacy, it's clear that children play and experiment with written language long before they reach first grade. We find that with the computer, this play and experimentation is enriched as never before. Let's look now at specific programs to see how they fit with the stages of language development in young children.

How Computers Can Support Emergent Literacy

Computers, used as a medium for exploration, creative efforts, and practice, can stimulate young children's emergent literacy. Here are some ways this can occur:

■ Easy-to-use computer letter games such as *Kid's Stuff* (Stone), *Animal Alphabet and Other Things* (Random House), and *Fun From A to Z* (MECC) can help children of preschool age learn to **discriminate and recognize letters** as they seek keyboard letters to match those on the screen. Letter recognition activities also help children learn their way around the computer keyboard. On computers with appropriate speech attachments, a program like *Dr. Peet's Talk/Writer* (Hartley) allows children to hear the names of letters as they type them and thus begin to recognize letters aurally as well as visually. (Letter names, rather than sounds, are apparently the first clues

Easy-to-use computer letter games, such as Kid's Stuff, *can help children of pre-school age learn to discriminate and recognize letters as they seek keyboard letters to match those on the screen.*

emergent writers use when trying to write words—as when a child writes "y" for "why.")

■ Preschool and kindergarten children can **link words to pictures of objects** in familiar storybook fashion using *Richard Scarry's Best Electronic Word Book Ever!* (Mindscape). Words flash and pictures animate as children guide Lowly Worm through farm, con-

struction, and railroad settings. Using MECC's *Paint With Words*, kindergarten children can create everyday scenes by moving words like "car," "boy," and "dog" into a scene where they are transformed into images of the referents.

■ Children can **explore words and their meanings** in action sentences with *Stickybear Reading* (Weekly Reader). This program allows children to construct a simple sentence, such as "The cow jumps over the dog," and then observe an animated illustration of the sentence on the computer screen.

■ Using word-processing programs, children can either **type words and phrases or dictate a narrative to adults**, who can then turn the dictation into print. Word processors, such as *Magic Slate* and *Muppet Slate* (both Sunburst), *The Bank Street Writer III* (Scholastic), *Dr. Peet's Talk/Writer* (Hartley), *Talking Textwriter* (Scholastic), and *FirstWriter* (Houghton Mifflin), use large letters (20 fill a line) that are easy for young children to recognize and read. They are thus ideally suited to taking dictation for individual or group language experiences. *Dr. Peet's Talk/Writer*, *Talking Textwriter*, and *FirstWriter* even pronounce words as they are typed and can read an entire story in a synthesized voice (box, p. 64).

Using word-processing programs, children can type words and phrases. Some programs even pronounce words as children type them and can read an entire story back in a synthesized voice.

A Child's Writing Session With Talking Textwriter

Leah is a kindergartner. She and several of her classmates were gathered around a computer one day to learn how to use *Talking Textwriter* (Scholastic), a program that pronounces letters and words as they are typed. The teacher had set up the program on the computer so that children could both type and listen. Each child tried a few letters, typing them and listening as the synthesized voice pronounced the letters.

After the introduction, Leah decided to stay at the computer and work with the program for a while. She began by typing her name and some other children's names that she knew. Leah demonstrated a major advance in her typing skills by typing a space between the names rather than running them into one another. (Typing a space between words is especially important with *Talking Textwriter* and other talking word processors, since the programs pronounce a word only after a space has been inserted to indicate that the word is completed.)

After a few moments, Leah looked away from the computer towards a poster on the classroom wall. She began typing afresh. First she typed a few letters, and then she looked a few more times at the poster, and then she typed a few more letters. When the teacher asked her what she was doing, she replied, "I'm typing that word because I want to know what it is!" Leah had created a game for herself—typing words she saw around the room to hear how they sounded! One of the words Leah found to type was "cricket," which she saw on top of the Cricket speech synthesizer (made by Street Electronics). When she heard the computer pronounce "cricket," it inspired her to write a story about a cricket. As she typed each word, she tried various letter combinations to achieve the sounds she wanted. Leah arrived at some nonstandard spellings, but since she could hear the letter combinations immediately transformed to speech, her spellings approximated standard spellings and often demonstrated a phonetic logic. This is what she finally wrote: "The cricket went faw a wok. He kame two his hous."

Leah's story is a short one and has a number of peculiar "words," but by writing it, she began to see herself as a writer.

Language Packages for Kindergartners

Young children's easy adaptation to using the computer as a language tool has inspired producers to offer computer program "packages" that span the language arts curriculum, including phonics, reading comprehension, and writing. Both the Apple Computer company and IBM Educational Systems have offerings of this type that are designed for early elementary grades, including kindergarten. IBM's *Writing to Read* is most frequently installed in a computer laboratory setting. Apple's package, part of its *Early Learning Series*, is intended for integration within the classroom and thus fits with our view of the computer as an integral part of the young child's classroom learning environment.

Apple's Classroom Approach

Apple's reading and writing package is designed for use in kindergarten, first grade, and second grade. The Apple package combines software and computer attachments (from a variety of vendors) with a teacher's manual and a voucher for training by Apple staff. This combination of software, computer attachments, manual, and training costs about $1,200, a little less than the total retail cost of just the software and attachments. When implemented with classroom computers, color monitors, and a printer, the package provides an instructional system consisting of three classroom learning stations—a skills station, a writing station, and a sound station. (Each station requires an Apple IIe or IIGS computer and a color monitor; these and the printer, of course, are not included in the $1,200 package price.)

The skills station is designed to introduce children to letters, words, and the reading readiness skills of sequencing and visual matching. Using a computer equipped with Muppet Learning Keys and a mouse, it employs the three Sunburst programs *Muppets On Stage*, *Muppetville*, and *Muppet Word Book*. The first and simplest of these programs, *Muppets On Stage*, introduces letters and numbers and helps children learn computer keys associated with them. In *Muppetville* and *Muppet Word Book*, children engage in such activities as matching shapes, colors, letters, numbers, and even musical phrases.

The writing station's computer is equipped with an Echo speech synthesizer (Street Electronics) and employs Scholastic's *Talking Textwriter* program, with its immediate and unlimited conversion of typed text to speech sounds. Thus the writing station is a place where children can explore the relationship between written text and speech sounds. If the station's computer is connected to a printer, children can also print and take with them the products of their exploration at the writing station.

Materials for the writing station also include the Sunburst *Touch 'N Write* program and a touch screen, which children can use to practice printing by tracing letters on the screen with a finger. The program gives children immediate feedback on the accuracy of each stroke of the finger.

The sound station is designed for systematic development of phonics skills. Also using a speech synthesizer connected to a computer, this station, at the kindergarten level, employs Houghton Mifflin's *Sound Ideas: Consonants* program. Organized around the key consonant sounds, the program's synthesized voice asks children to "find the picture name that begins with the same sound as monkey," for example. Children select a match from three possible choices. The strength of the phonics exercises of *Sound Ideas* lies in the immediate feedback provided by the computer and its synthesized speech.

The two-pronged emphasis of the Apple package—on exploratory, creative writing and on phonics instruction—is similar to the emphasis of the IBM package, *Writing to Read*.

IBM's Lab Approach

As mentioned earlier, IBM's package is presently designed for use in a computer laboratory that is separate from the classroom. (We have seen it adapted to use within the classroom however.) In addition to computer activities, the *Writing to Read* laboratory contains a listening area; a manipulative area with clay, chalk, and stencils for tactile experiences with letter shapes; a center for word games; and a writing center with typewriters, computers, and paper and pencil for story writing.

The *Writing to Read* program, according to its developer John Henry Martin, teaches kindergartners and first graders to write and spell words and sentences and to create stories—on their own. The program's "talking" computer uses computer pictures and computer-synthesized speech to teach simple spelling rules that allow young children in as little as 20 weeks to spell virtually all the 2000 words in their speaking vocabulary.

The heart of the *Writing to Read* concept is its phonemic alphabet—42 sound/symbol pairs, like the "c" in "cat," the long "ē" in "me," the "ow" in "cow," and the "air" in "fair." Using the system, a kindergarten child wrote the following story:

"Crystal ī love you. that diamn ī gav you wuz not rel."

One can see that *Writing to Read* rules do not always yield standard spellings. For example, the long "ā" with a macron bar above is used to spell "vās" (a cup to hold flowers) without the final, silent "e." Rules like these greatly simplify the young child's task of putting words into print. Yet, children are constantly exposed to standard spellings in *Writing to Read* materials, which present both phonetic and standard spellings, and by reading (or following listening-center tapes of) familiar storybooks that use only standard spellings. The idea is that children will spell phonetically as they start to write, but gradually switch to standard spellings as they grow older. In addition, children can mix *Writing to Read* and standard spellings in their own writings. The Educational Testing Service's evaluation of *Writing to Read* suggests that *Writing to Read* children, besides writing and reading better than their non-*Writing to Read* peers, also use standard spelling at least as well.

Computer Effects in Kindergarten

F ew studies, to date, have demonstrated clear-cut effects of computers on the learning of children as young as kindergarten age. The study of *Writing to Read* effects by the Educational Testing Service is one of the few. Another series of studies from Stanford University shows how computers and a variety of off-the-shelf software programs affect the school readiness skills of kindergarten children.

The studies were conducted in 1986 in the public schools in the Palo Alto area under the direction of Robert Hess, a professor of education at Stanford. Kindergarten classrooms in three schools were provided sufficient IBM PCjr computers to maintain a ratio of no more than six students to each computer. Kindergartners in two additional schools without classroom computers served as comparisons. In the computer classrooms, teachers arranged classroom schedules to allow each child at least one hour per week at the computer. In addition, families of one group of kindergartners received a PCjr for home use and were able to borrow copies of the programs their children were using in school. The software used in the study included such programs as *Easy as ABC* (Springboard) and *Reader Rabbit* (Learning Co.), in other words, programs familiar to many computer-using preschool and kindergarten teachers.

Children were tested at the beginning of the year, prior to computer use, and again at the end of the year, to determine what effects, if any, the computers had on their learning. The tests included, among other things, items that represented overall curriculum goals in the area of reading readiness.

The results of the study regarding reading readiness are impressive. Kindergarten children using computers improved their scores in reading readiness by 16 percent from fall to spring—significantly more than the comparison children's 6 percent improvement. The group that used computers at home as well as at school gained even more, improving their reading readiness scores by nearly 52 percent.

Researchers also reported generally positive effects of computers on the social and emotional climate of the classroom, saying that the computers stimulated even more positive social interaction than did other materials in the classroom. The study also demonstrated that teachers, working by themselves in self-contained classrooms, were able to successfully incorporate computer learning.

With younger and younger children using computers for writing, we face the unavoidable question of when and how to introduce keyboard skills.

Is Touch-Typing Next?

The existence of systems like Apple's *Early Learning Series* and IBM's *Writing to Read* means that younger and younger children are using computers for writing. Thus we face the unavoidable questions of when and how to introduce keyboard skills—skills that involve rapid and accurate typing, with minimal conscious attention, on standard typewriter and computer keyboards.

Fortunately, since most young children don't have the eye-hand coordination or fine-motor skills necessary for extensive typing, many early childhood computer programs require use of just a few keys (the spacebar and RETURN, for example), or they elimi-

nate using the keyboard altogether, in favor of using a joystick or mouse. Though children may sometimes need practice or special help to develop even such simple input skills, they usually pick them up as required in the context of the computer activity.

However, children do not as easily develop the keyboard skills necessary for complex writing activities, when most of the writer's attention must be focused on content; people rarely develop this so-called touch-typing without a systematic effort. Though older students should be concerned about engaging in such a systematic effort at some point if they are to benefit from the advantages of the computer, how early such an effort *can* be undertaken or *should* be undertaken is, in our minds, an open question.

Some educators argue that touch-typing instruction should begin in kindergarten, so the bad habits of hunt-and-peck do not become barriers to learning touch-typing in later grades. Acting on this belief, a kindergarten typing project at the Bernardsville Public Schools in New Jersey used nail polishes and correspondingly colored keys to develop kindergartners' familiarity with fingering of the home-row letters ASDF and JKL;. Kindergartners so instructed could accurately type simple words and sentences in blindfold tests.

Many early childhood professionals question the wisdom of such early systematic touch-typing instruction, however, since educators now generally agree that the spirit of initial writing instruction should be to encourage children to write by minimizing inhibitions. Though early introduction of computers fits this spirit by simplifying the child's task of letter formation, an early emphasis on learning touch-typing could inhibit children's interest in writing in much the same way that an early emphasis on learning spelling, punctuation, or cursive writing might do so.

For kindergartners who are beginning to type words or sentences, and perhaps even short stories or poems, any introduction to touch-typing should, at most, be this:

■ Guiding children to use both hands to hunt-and-peck, so that they begin to cover the left side of the keyboard with one hand and the right side with the other hand

■ Highlighting in some way the home-row, and perhaps even the home-keys, so children using the hunt-and-peck method might use these as a starting point for their hands

Most likely, until they are well along in the middle grades, children will not be typing enough words to justify learning the touch-typing method. Any long stories preschoolers and kindergartners write will probably be a group effort, in which an adult does the touch-typing while children take turns dictating their contributions to the story.

"Language Experience" Stories by Computer

Writing group stories during circle time or other group periods is an activity we promised to talk more about when we mentioned it in connection with daily computer use, in Chapter 3. You may recall our earlier description of group-dictated stories—often called language experience stories—that relate to a class field trip or to special themes, such as a holiday or "our families."

The language experience story is created as each child narrates his or her part for the group while an adult types at the computer. The dictation appears on the screen as it is being typed, and each child's name is included in the text just above the part he or she has dictated. The adult may read back each child's episode from the screen and incorporate on the spot any changes the child wishes to make. Later, children can experience "being published"—teachers can print, copy, and send home the complete story to be read by children with their parents.

The word processing program *Magic Slate* (Sunburst) is one we've found well suited to group dictation projects. The program's picture menu makes it very easy to use. *Magic Slate* letters are about ¾-inch high on the screen and almost ½-inch high when printed. If the program's largest letters are used, 20 of them fill a line, making the lines short and visible to a group of young children. The program also has many features that make it easy for a teacher to go back, once a dictation session is completed, to correct typing errors, enter the authors' names, and tidy up spacings for the final printed product.

Another program to consider for group dictation projects is *Language Experience Recorder Plus* (Teacher Support). We mention this program because it is able to compute a variety of useful statistics describing the text children dictate. It can compute readability level, average sentence-length, average word-length, word count, and proportion of unique words. The program will also produce an alphabetized word-list showing the frequency of each word used by children in their dictation. Such statistics provide an objective way to assess the complexity of children's language, which could be a boon for preschool and kindergarten teachers who wish to track individual children's language development without resorting to worksheet counts or standardized testing.

```
              THE PARK
MIRIAM
        We went to the park. We
walked.
JAMAL
        We went to the slides.
AMBER H.
        We went on the swings.
AMBER B.
        We went to go see the pond.
GREGORY
        I played with the ball.
CHRIS S.
        At the pond we found some
sticks, and we got a hockey
stick.
KAHLIL
        We played basketball.
LAURA
        We played on the bridge.
THE LAST THING
        We had one more turn on the
swings and slides. Then we went
back to school.
        THE END
```

A language experience story one class wrote using Magic Slate

Summary

In this chapter, we have illustrated a variety of ways that computers can fit into the natural language learning processes of young children. Many of the programs and techniques described foster children's independence, allow them to make choices, and encourage them to convert their spoken language skills into literacy and creative expression. If appropriate language software is employed, the computer can truly become the children's "scaffold" for their climb from emergent literacy towards language competence. In the next chapter, we describe ways the computer supports children's efforts to explore the world of logic and mathematics.

5 Computers and Young Children's Logical/Mathematical Thinking

We debated whether we should title this chapter simply Computers and Math Development, but we realized that a large portion of young children's software—that is, much of the software *not* dealing with language development—really covers a category broader than numbers and counting. We have dubbed this broader category "logical/mathematical thinking" to include, for example, children's experiences with identifying and classifying objects, putting a set of objects in order, and comparing sets by putting them in one-to-one correspondence. We also include children's ability to derive ideas of quantity or number from their comparison and ordering experiences, as well as their ability to use number words and symbols to talk about these new ideas. Finally, we include children's experiences of spatial relationships—size, position, shape— and of temporal relationships.

We're talking, of course, about abilities children develop and exercise every day in play with familiar materials— when they sort beads and blocks by size or shape, when they line up their trucks or teddy bears by size, when they match drivers to race cars or cups to saucers, when they take apart and put together puzzles, and when they sing counting songs as they walk up steps. Now there's another "material" they can use to exercise and develop their logical/mathematical abilities— the computer.

Computers and logical/mathematical thinking have been closely associated since the early days of the computing machines. Mathematicians, like John Napier (who in 1614 introduced logarithms, the basis of the slide rule) and Charles Babbage (who developed the idea of a mechanical digital computer in the 1830s), were naturally interested in mechanization to ease the toil of long calculations. In 1945 the mathematician John von Neumann laid out in detail the key components of the modern digital computer.

Considering the computer's development by mathematicians, it's not surprising that one of its first educational applications was in the area of arithmetic skills instruction; given their computational abilities, computers could easily verify children's answers to arithmetic problems. However, these early computer programs for teaching arithmetic skills primarily offered drill-and-practice on traditional "math facts"—not so appropriate in educating younger children.

Though drill and practice in varied formats remains a popular computer function, educational computer programs have moved into areas more suitable for early childhood. Exploiting the computer's ability to present animated pictures and to respond interactively, today's programs for young children provide games, puzzles, and creative activities that help youngsters develop such logical/mathematical skills as sorting, ordering, comparing, and counting. They also allow children to explore (within the limits of a two-dimensional presentation) the concepts of size, position, and location. When such programs as these are available, preschool and kindergarten children use them as readily and enjoyably as they use manipulative puzzles, games, and building materials. In this chapter, we examine in detail several aspects of children's logical/mathematical thinking and describe some computer programs designed to provide experiences with such thinking.

Classification Experiences With the Computer

For adults, classifying involves such experiences as knowing where to look for sauerkraut in a supermarket or where to look for a used hubcap in the yellow pages; but this ability to classify has also led to such complex developments as the periodic table of elements and the taxonomy of the plant and animal kingdoms. Classification experiences begin in childhood, as youngsters begin to notice similarities and differences in the shape, size, sound, color, taste, smell, feel, and use of objects. Such early experiences are an important part of a child's developing logical/mathematical capabilities.

For the preschool child, early classification experiences should involve hands-on exploration of real objects. However, computers can also provide a young child with experiences in recognizing similarities and differences, and they can provide valuable feedback to a child who is exploring attributes of two-dimensional on-screen images.

A young child can learn about shapes, colors, and sizes—all easily displayed two-dimensionally—by searching visually for matching shapes, colors, or sizes in a set of objects shown on a computer screen. The success of such searching can be confirmed through sounds or pictures generated by the computer when a match is found. *Colors and Shapes* (Hartley), *Observation and Classification* (Hartley), and *Easy Street* (Mindplay) are examples of programs that provide game-like contexts for matching shapes, colors, and sizes at a level suitable for preschool children. In each of these programs, children select a matching item from one of several choices pictured on the screen or identify an object that does not belong in a group.

In addition to noting similarities and differences and identifying objects that don't belong in a set, many kindergarten and some preschool children are able to *group* objects on the basis of similarities of color, shape, size, use, weight, and other attributes, and they are able to relate these groups to one another. For example, given a set of red, blue, and yellow objects shaped as squares, triangles, and diamonds, kindergarten children can sort out a group of squares, of triangles, or of diamonds, or they can sort out a group of reds, of blues, or of yellows.

A similar sorting game can be played using the computer program *Gertrude's Secrets* (Learning Co.). In Gertrude's "one-loop" puzzles, for example, a child tries to determine what pieces (of a certain shape or color) Gertrude the goose has "secretly" chosen to include inside this loop. The child picks pieces from the set of shapes and colors and moves them into the loop, using the arrow keys or joystick. If the pieces meet Gertrude's secret criterion for inclusion, they remain in the loop. If they do not meet Gertrude's criterion, they fall to the bottom of the screen. Proceeding in this way, by noting what type of piece tends to remain in the loop, children complete the puzzle by placing all pieces of Gertrude's chosen color or shape inside the loop.

Children can play a challenging sorting game using the computer program Gertrude's Secrets.

How Computers Help With Spatial Concepts

Every time we wrap a package, consult a map, or frame a picture, we are using our understanding of spatial relationships to solve problems. It is easy for adults to take for granted an understanding of spatial relationships, but children need years of experience and learning to develop an understanding of these basic concepts.

Children's learning about space begins early in life with the grasping and manipulation of objects and intensifies as the child begins moving through space by crawling and walking. By early childhood, children can distinguish a variety of geometric shapes from one another. They also understand a variety of positional relationships, such as *on*, *in*, *next to*, *in front of*. They can make simple drawings of objects and people, and they can construct a great variety of buildings and other structures from blocks, Tinkertoys, and Legos. They are also able to recognize objects from a variety of visual perspectives, although they cannot yet identify or describe objects as someone else might see them.

Two key spatial experiences in early childhood are

■ Taking apart and fitting together pieces that make a whole

■ Experiencing and describing relative positions, directions, and distances—*inside*, *outside*, *above*, *below*, *before*, *behind*, *on*, *under*, *toward*, *away*, *far*, *near*

Children's acquaintance with these experiences in early childhood leads to later, more complex spatial abilities, such as being able to understand maps, measurement, and visual perspective. Although these experiences occur primarily when children move things about, build, measure, and represent spatial relationships in words and drawings, computers can also provide some—though not all—of the important spatial experiences in activities that are fun for young children. This section describes computer programs dealing with the two key experiences just listed.

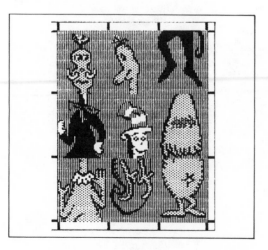

A screen dump showing a puzzle from Dr. Seuss Fix-Up the Mix-up Puzzler

In this introductory activity to a computerized puzzle, a child assembles a similar puzzle that his teacher has made from a magazine illustration.

Taking Apart and Putting Together Parts of a Whole

Children learn about the spatial relationships among the parts of a whole by taking things apart and putting them back together. Blocks, take-apart toys, and puzzles are popular materials for this kind of learning. To a limited extent, computer activities can also provide children with such experiences. Computerized puzzle games, such as CBS Software's *Dr. Seuss Fix-Up the Mix-Up Puzzler*, enable children to assemble puzzles that can be re-divided by the computer in a new way each time the game is played. These

programs can also vary the difficulty level of a puzzle by dividing it into more or fewer pieces. Another advantage computer puzzles have over conventional puzzles is that the pieces can't get lost.

Experiencing Positions, Directions, and Distances

An adult's understanding of position, direction, and distance are all brought

By early childhood, children can understand a variety of positional relationships. This computer program illustrates "near" for a child.

to bear in an experience such as operating a motor vehicle along a designated map route. Again, the beginnings of understanding such concepts may be found in early childhood. Children learn about positions and directions by moving about and handling objects in their environment and by talking about these experiences with others. Relationships of position and direction confront children in many ways: They get burned if they are too close to a hot object; a cookie in the hand (nearby) is worth two in the jar (far away); turning a water faucet one way turns water on, while turning it the other way turns water off.

Computers can also help children learn about position and direction. For example, preschool children can experience directionality as they use a mouse or a joystick to guide an electronic crayon in a drawing program such as *Color Me* (Mindscape). Preschool children also enjoy the directional challenge of similarly guiding gondolas through the canals of Venice to rescue ducks from a lurking Hippo in *Ducks Ahoy!* (Joyce Hakansson). (See the discussion of *Ducks Ahoy!* in Chapter 6.)

Older preschool and kindergarten children can navigate a car on a map of their favorite town with the program *Stickybear Town Builder* (Weekly

Reader). Also at the kindergarten level, programs like *Delta Drawing* (Spinnaker) and *EZ Logo* (MECC) give the direction commands *forward*, *backward*, *right* and *left* specific meanings that children can explore. These programs enable children to draw on the computer screen by typing a word or letter command (for example, FORWARD or F) to move the cursor in a desired direction.

How Computers Contribute to Order and Pattern Concepts

Part of children's developing logical/mathematical ability has to do with understanding order and patterns. In the older child, ordering ability means being able to organize a set of fractions, for example, from least to greatest, or to locate "bin" in the dictionary by looking after "bean" but before "boat." But ordering begins for preschoolers simply with feeling and experiencing differences in size, weight, temperature, texture, color, and then talking about what is more or less, taller or shorter, rougher or smoother, before or after. For preschool children, ordering ability involves three key experiences:

- Making comparisons

- Ordering a small number of objects and events

- Matching one ordered set to another

Ordering experiences for young children should of course include comparing real objects—seeing two crayons that are light and dark shades of the

same color, feeling rough and smooth textures of sandpaper, tasting sweet and bitter foods, hearing high- and low-pitched sounds. Preschoolers who show an awareness of such differences can then begin to put things in order: They might arrange three or four trucks from shortest to longest as they clean up the block area, or they might describe three events as "first," "next," and "last" as they review a morning's activities. They might match big plates with big dolls and small plates with small dolls as they pretend in the house area.

Kindergarten children (beginning to understand such words as "between") are increasingly aware of order relations and can systematically construct sequences and patterns with *more* than three or four objects. Key ordering experiences for them include

- Systematically ordering five or more objects or events

- Inserting items into a series that is already formed

Computer programs can play a part in helping children understand order. In some programs, understanding order is a crucial factor in playing a computer game; in others, children can explore on-screen patterns and sequences and receive computer feedback as they do so. One example of a program involving ordering is Hartley's *Patterns and Sequences*. Easy enough for preschoolers, the program's first activity, "Scratch Match," introduces children to the shapes used throughout *Patterns and Sequences* with a

A child sharpens his understanding of ordering by using this activity from Patterns and Sequences.

game in which children, given three alternatives, find a match for a given shape. Another preschool-level activity, "Ms. Bug," invites children to find a match for a sequence of two shapes. Kindergarten children can sharpen their understanding of ordering by using the "Train Game" and "Dan's Van" activities from *Patterns and Sequences*. Teachers can introduce the "Train Game," which employs three-shape patterns, by asking children to first make different three-shape patterns with beads and string. This is a good lead-in to the computer activity, in which children find a match for a three-shape sequence by choosing

from among three possible three-shape sequences.

Pattern building and pattern extending are other activities found in computer programs. The program *Patterns* (MECC), for example, enables children to create and print a pattern of their own or to build on a pattern that is already started. *Peter's Growing Patterns* (Strawberry Hill) has a similar pattern-completing activity.

Experience in ordering events, such as the progressive stages of a snowman melting, is provided by *1-2-3 Sequence Me* (Sunburst). This program does require understanding of the numerical order of 1, 2, and 3, however; so it is more appropriate for kindergartners than for preschoolers.

Kindergarten children can also enjoy a musical ordering task with a program called *Prokofiev's Peter and the Wolf: Music* (Spinnaker). In addition to identifying similar and different strains from the Prokofiev score, they also try to determine which of two pitches is higher; in another activity, they try to fit a duck between two others according to the pitch of its voice.

Computer Activities That Nurture a Basic Concept: One-to-One

Children place objects in **one-to-one correspondence** when they fill each hole in a pegboard with a peg; when they make a garage for each of several toy cars; or when they hang socks up to dry, matching one clothespin per sock. Passing out apples, one to a child, or covering both ears with your two hands are other everyday activities that involve one-to-one correspondence. Two sets of objects—like the cars and their garages—that correspond exactly, one-to-one, contain **the same number** of objects. Thus children's grasp of the meaning of **number** grows out of adequate experience with one-to-one matching in many different contexts.

Computers can be especially helpful by providing children with extended experience in one-to-one matching without moving them prematurely into counting. In *Conservation and Counting* (Hartley), children match sea

horses with sea plants, for example. In another program, *Counters* (an overall introduction to numbers and arithmetic by Sunburst), one activity has children using the computer's spacebar to match one set of animals, one-to-one, with another set. At the easiest level of matching, the animals in each set correspond very neatly with their "mates" in the other set, so that each duck in one set, for example, lines up neatly with one of the ducks in the other set. At a more advanced level of matching, objects to be matched one-to-one with those of another set are no longer placed in obvious correspondence. Rather, the second set is more spread out or bunched up than the first, thus contrasting *number* with *space occupied* and, by providing this challenge, bringing the child one step closer to a stable concept of number.

Computer Activities That Teach Counting, Number Names, and Number Concepts

Counting and Its Principles

Development of counting skills also plays a central role in children's understanding of early number concepts and in the subsequent development of arithmetic and measurement skills. Rochel Gelman and C. R. Gallistel in *The Child's Understanding of Number* (Harvard University Press, 1986) list five counting principles that children acquire during the preschool and kindergarten years:

1. Using just one tag (number name or other word) for each object

2. Using the tags in a stable order (always "one," "two," "three")

3. Using the last tag to describe the number in the set

4. Counting selectively (for example, just the cats in a set of animals)

5. Realizing that the order in which the objects are counted makes no difference

These counting principles tie in with many of the counting activities that are available in computer programs for young children. Many programs do a good job of *supporting* children's acquisition of the five counting principles, but these computer programs alone do not span all the principles. An adult still needs to

A Preliminary Activity for Counting Critters

The "Math Magic" activity in MECC's *Counting Critters* involves a magician's hat with different numbers of animals coming out of it. An effective way to introduce children to this activity is by showing them a real hat containing an assortment of small toy animals. Children might begin by reaching into this "magic hat" and describing what kinds of animals they feel inside the hat.

Then give each child a "magic hat" and a set of small animals to use with it in various ways. For example, some pairs of children might choose to be magicians and play a game in which one child puts some animals in the hat and the other child guesses how many animals are in the hat. Then both children check the guess by counting the animals as they take them out of the hat. Other children might choose to work alone, counting animals as they put them in or take them out of the hat. Some children will choose to wear their hats while they devise some other type of play with their toy animals. You can support the children's various activities by asking them number questions about the animals that are in or out of their hats.

While the children are playing with their hats and animals, turn the computer on to the "Math Magic" activity and call children's attention to the "magic hat" on the screen. Demonstrate how to make the animals come out of the on-screen hat and how children can use the computer to count the animals. After everyone who is interested has had a chance to try this computer version of playing with a "magic hat," let children know when "Math Magic" will be in the computer area for their use at work time.

model the use of the *spoken* tags "one," "two," "three." With a tag system available to them, children can then count sets of objects or people in the classroom as well as items on the computer screen. Adults also need to model the one-to-one matching of tags to objects, to help children realize that items are counted just once.

Counting Critters (MECC) is a program that introduces young children to many of the counting ideas (see box). In this program, children identify matching numerals, do simple counting, and learn numerical order in enjoyable and easy-to-use game formats.

Number Farm (DLM) is another good all-around introduction to numbers for preschool and kindergarten children. The program contains activities for counting and estimating, as well as a number-guessing game introducing the concepts of **greater than** and **less than**.

One counting activity involves counting sounds, like the barks of a dog and the moos of a cow.

For a program concentrating on counting, there's Sunburst's *Counters*. The program presents counting in a Piagetian sequence, starting with the concept of one-to-one correspondence (as described in the previous section), then moving to the concept of number.

C&C Software's *Learning About Numbers* also concentrates on counting, but it skips preliminary concepts and starts with simple counting. One feature of this program, however, is its ability to keep track of the counting skills of each child who uses it.

Number Patterns and Relationships

Counting can be a road leading children to an understanding of the concept of number during the pre-

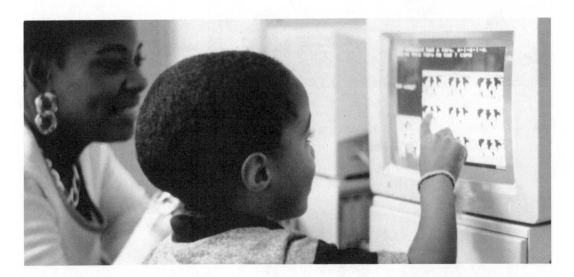

Number Farm *emphasizes number patterns in a counting activity that employs a 3×3 grid and shows sets of objects arrayed in various ways within that grid.*

school years, but counting should not be the *only* avenue of approach to arithmetic skills. Good computer programs for math development also emphasize **number patterns** (the smaller sets within larger sets of objects, for example) and **number relationships**, such as *more than*, *less than*, and *the same as*. (Youngsters who never get beyond counting to determine number or to determine sums and differences may have difficulty mastering more advanced arithmetic skills.) But counting seems to be a child's first handle on solving problems involving number and a fall-back procedure (once others have developed) to which he or she returns periodically as sets increase in size and mathematical operations increase in complexity.

Math Rabbit (Learning Co.) emphasizes number meanings and number

The program Numbers *varies the counting process in several well-designed balloon-popping activities.*

A screen dump from Numbers. *In this activity, children continue popping balloons (after the computer has popped 3) until 6 balloons have been popped in all.*

patterns in a "Music Maker" game that gives the numbers 1 through 8 musical interpretations (by using higher and lower tones). There is also a matching activity, "Tightrope," where sets of objects are made to fall from the tightrope if they do not match a greater-than, less-than, or equal-to criterion. Even the *Math Rabbit* game introducing addition and subtraction employs patterns by presenting children with sums like $2+1$, $2+2$, $2+3$, and so on, in an ordered sequence.

Number Farm (DLM) emphasizes number patterns in a counting activity called "Crop Count." The activity employs a 3×3 grid and shows sets of countable objects arrayed in various ways within that grid. Thus children count five objects, for example, arrayed in different ways, so that 5 takes on more and more meaning for them. In a similar fashion, *Counting Critters* (MECC) provides countable sets of jungle animals arranged in various ways.

Numbers (Lawrence) varies the counting process in several well-designed balloon-popping activities to include the counting of the sets and subsets involved in addition and subtraction.

Addition and Subtraction Action

Some kindergartners, working independently, may proceed as far as the addition and subtraction activities provided by computer programs. Therefore, you should know that some programs dealing with addition and subtraction are better than others. In general, those that use animation to emphasize the **joining or separating action** associated with adding or subtracting are most appropriate for an introduction to these operations. The "Muppet Factory" activity in *Muppetville* (Sunburst) does a good job of showing such action, as does *1st Math* (Stone). Also, programs that relate the added or subtracted numbers to **sets of objects** are better than those that provide only "symbol juggling." The Sunburst program *Counters*, for example, provides countable sets alongside

For the kindergartner who proceeds as far as arithmetic operations, those computer programs that use animation to emphasize the joining action associated with addition are best.

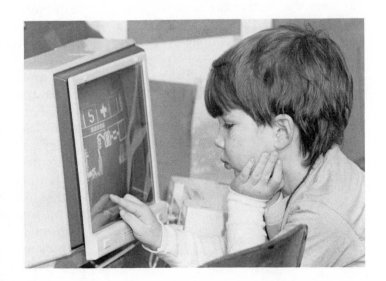

its addition and subtraction problems, to aid children in the transition from sets of objects to number facts.

Other types of addition and subtraction programs, those more suited to children beyond kindergarten, provide symbolic-level drill-and-practice activities embedded in motivational games. *Learning About Numbers* (C&C) is such a program. In addition to providing a clever troll, prince, and heroine game involving addition and subtraction facts, it includes teacher options for tailoring the content selection and difficulty level to the needs of each child. It also unobtrusively tracks individual children's progress.

The Beginnings of Measurement

By the time children are in kindergarten, they are interested in comparing objects with one another and they are keenly aware that some objects are bigger (or smaller) than others. They also enjoy counting and can count the blocks in the wall of one building, for example, to determine whether it is longer than another wall. In other words, they are beginning to use nonstandard units of measurement. The computer can give children a chance to explore this concept.

Estimation (Lawrence) provides easily understood situations in which children can compare lines to determine which one is longer. It also asks them to estimate how many bugs will match the length of a line or how many trucks will fill a jar. The program pro-

vides feedback on these estimations that is nonthreatening and thus encourages children to make better and better judgments.

Fish Scales (DLM) introduces concepts of length and measurement for kindergarten and older children in delightful games with various-sized fish.

Computer Experiences With Time

Many preschool and kindergarten children cannot yet tell time, but this doesn't mean they have no understanding of temporal relationships. For example, through the daily classroom routine, they know something about the order of events: Snack time comes after clean-up time. They can start an activity on a signal and they can stop on another. They can distinguish between fast and slow rates of activity. Early childhood educators can help young children strengthen these emerging skills to a point where telling time makes sense. In particular, the skill of starting and stopping an action on signal can be strengthened with children's use of the computer program *Estimation*, which we mentioned in the previous section.

Estimation offers an appealing activity, "Choo-Choo," in which preschool and kindergarten children stop an animated train when it reaches a marker on the tracks. Children's sense of time—and timing—plays a major role in their success at this game. This computer activity can be used along with other start-and-stop activities—races, marches (starting and stopping to music), and the use of a timer to aid turn-taking, all of which provide varied experiences in starting and stopping activities on a signal (see box).

A Preliminary Activity for Estimation's "Choo-Choo"

Before trying the "Choo-Choo" activity with your children, talk with them about "start" and "stop." For example, during circle time, children might start and stop walking or moving to music. Also, in a separate small-group activity, you might tie a string to a small toy train and pull it along a table top. Then ask individual children to start the train by saying "start" and to stop the train by saying "stop." Start and stop the train as each child commands. Then place an arrow on the table. Pull the train along the table and ask the children to say "stop" when the train reaches the arrow. Invite a child-volunteer to pull the train towards the arrow while the other children stop the train by saying "stop" when the train reaches the arrow.

As the children demonstrate a grasp of stopping the three-dimensional train on signal, turn the computer on to the "Choo-Choo" activity from *Estimation*. Demonstrate how the spacebar starts and stops the train. Start the train on a signal from the children and ask them to tell you to stop the train when it reaches the arrow. After the group has had several successes stopping the train at the arrow, invite children either individually or in pairs to try starting the train and then stopping it just as it reaches the arrow.

Preschoolers can become quite adept at stopping the train at the arrow. The "Choo-Choo" activity retains its appeal; children will continue to practice starting and stopping the train for weeks if the activity is available to them in the computer area.

Introduce kindergartners to the train activity with a three-dimensional train, but make a tunnel for the train with several blocks. Place an arrow close to the middle of the tunnel; then pull the train through the tunnel and ask the kindergartners to tell you to stop the train when they think it has reached the arrow. Then start the computer activity, asking the children to say "stop" when they think the train in the tunnel has reached the arrow. Play the game several more times as a group. Then let children in pairs or alone take turns starting and stopping the train on the computer screen. After the small-group introduction to the train activity, encourage the kindergartners to use it on their own.

Although an awareness of the clock and its function begins in early childhood, telling time from clocks and performing time calculations using clock arithmetic are unsuitable for children of preschool and kindergarten age. Young children can, however, begin to grasp the relationship between movement, time, and speed, and they enjoy using such timing devices as sand timers and kitchen timers. When clock reading is appropriate, at the first- or second-grade level, several computer programs can provide practice with reading or setting the clock, including *Clock Works* (MECC) and *Learning About Numbers (C&C)*.

Summary

Young children themselves have proved that the logical/mathematical computer programs described in this chapter are enjoyable to use. The program activities are more varied and interesting and, above all, more interactive than the worksheets traditionally used to introduce children to logical/mathematical thinking. Having found them adaptable to preschoolers' and kindergartners' individual tastes and levels of ability, we recommend them not as a substitute for but as a supplement to other early childhood active learning experiences. In the next chapter, we discuss some computer-related curriculum topics that fall outside of the traditional areas of language development and logical/mathematical development.

⑥ Other Curriculum-Related Topics

Certain topics that don't fit easily into traditional curricular "pigeon holes" have come up in the course of our computer work, often during interactions among participants in our computer workshops. For example, workshop participants want to know about the value of computer drawing activities for children or about ways that computer programs encourage children's creativity. Topics our participants haven't thought of, we have: how computers provide cause-and-effect experiences, how computers assist with memory development, and how important "computer literacy" is for young children. In this final chapter, we offer our thoughts on these diverse topics.

Computer-Generated Artwork

One important area of adult computer use is computer-assisted drawing and "painting." Not just for scientific and technical use, this "computer art" is beginning to take its place alongside other reputable art forms. In particular, the computer is rapidly becoming a flexible and commercially important medium for graphic art and animation. Teachers sometimes express curiosity about computer art activity for chil-

dren, since several programs available for young children are marketed as "drawing" or "coloring" programs. We find that just as the computer allows children to explore language, logic, and quantity, it also allows them to explore the elements of drawing.

In our view, there is one outstanding computer program that allows pre-schoolers and kindergartners to experiment with line, color, and composition on the computer screen in much the same way that they might explore these elements by using paints, markers, or crayons on various kinds of materials and surfaces. (In fact, one small-group activity we use to introduce computer drawing consists of first providing children with a variety of pens, markers, chalk, and crayons and a variety of surfaces to use them on.) The outstanding program we're referring to, *Color Me* (Mindscape), has an easy-to-use menu (which some other drawing programs lack) and can be used with the Koala Pad, mouse, or joystick for drawing lines. (Our preference is the mouse, since it's widely available and children easily adapt to

Children can experiment with line, color, and composition on the computer screen in much the same way that they might explore these elements by using other media.

the hand motion involved.) Other relatively easy-to-use drawing programs include C&C Software's *Magic Crayon* (which employs the joystick to draw lines) and Spinnaker's *Kindercomp*

(which employs the arrow keys to draw lines).

All these programs allow children to **draw lines** by moving the cursor, which leaves a trail of color behind.

One Child's Mastery of Color Me

Paul is a small, reserved four-year-old in our preschool. Since entering the program as a three-year-old, he has displayed considerable interest in the computers. In his reserved manner, however, he usually lets others take the leading role at the computer while he simply watches. Recently, Paul demonstrated just how much he has absorbed while taking a back seat at the computer.

When we observed him, Paul was working alone, using Mindscape's *Color Me*. It wasn't the drawing Paul was creating that seemed so remarkable. Rather, it was the way he went about working on his drawing that was of interest.

Until now, Paul's experience with *Color Me* had been through observing others use the program. He also had a brief introduction to the program in small group. But none of this prior experience would seem to account for Paul's facility with the program—in particular for the extraordinary number of drawing tools he was so confidently using to make his picture. Paul was deliberately and purposefully using each feature of the program:

First he drew several lines of one color, using the draw function, a mouse-controlled "crayon." Then he selected another color from the "paintbox" and drew several more lines of the new color. After trying several colors in this way, he experimented with different "brush sizes," selecting first a medium, then a large, then a fine point, and finally selecting the "air brush" (to produce an airy, spray-painted effect). After that he began to use the fill function to create spots of color in the field of his drawing. (This is more complex than it sounds, since the function must be started and then stopped in time to avoid filling the whole screen with one color.)

When all this was done, Paul began to erase parts of his drawing by setting the mouse-controlled crayon's color to that of the background (in this case, white) and then drawing over those items he wanted to erase, which effectively whited them out. When this proved too slow a process for Paul's purposes, he moved the mouse-controlled pointer to the "erase page" option (depicted by a pencil, eraser-end down), and with a click, he erased the entire screen. Then, starting from scratch, he created another picture in the same methodical and proficient fashion.

Many children Paul's age enjoy using *Color Me*, but they usually learn how to use its various features one at a time, over a long period. For weeks, Paul had apparently been storing up nearly everything he observed other children doing with the program. Then, in one 20-minute hands-on session, he began to use his silently mastered *Color Me* skills.

Using one of the various input devices just mentioned—joystick, mouse, Koala Pad, arrow keys—children can direct the cursor around the screen and thus produce trails (lines) going in various directions to compose desired patterns, shapes, or pictures. As we mentioned in Chapter 2, the type of input device used determines what kinds of lines are most easily drawn: The mouse and Koala Pad more closely approximate free-hand drawing, with curves and irregular lines, whereas the arrow keys and joystick facilitate straight-line drawing, with horizontal and vertical lines.

Drawing programs allow children to **experiment with color** not only by producing lines in various colors but also by providing a "fill tool" for coloring areas of the screen or for coloring shapes that have been drawn. Children select in various ways the color they want to use—by typing either a letter or name or by moving the cursor to a "paint pot" or a "color bar." On an empty screen, the fill tool will cover the entire screen with a selected color, or if the filling is halted at a certain point, it will create just a splash of color. Preschool children using *Color Me* with a mouse control enjoy creating designs

It's important to be able to print a child's computer art, so it can be taken home or shared with others.

A child's drawing created with Color Me

made up of these color splashes. The swooshing sound that accompanies use of the fill tool in *Color Me* adds to their enjoyment (box, p. 91).

Although *Color Me* is available for the Apple, Commodore, and IBM computers, and the other drawing programs we've mentioned are also available for more than one system, it's interesting to note that the colors used in a given drawing program may vary from system to system—in intensity, variety, and saturation. This may be something to check out before you select a drawing program for use with your system. Also, the importance of being able to print a child's computer art, so it can be taken home or shared with others, is comparable to the importance of being able to print children's stories. Thus, having a classroom printer, especially a color printer, greatly enhances children's computer art activities.

Other computer drawing programs of note are the *Koala Pad Graphics Exhibitor* (PTI/Koala), *Deluxe Paint* (Electronic Arts), and *MacPaint* (CLARIS), but these programs are generally too complex for independent use by young children. Some children's

"art" programs are the equivalent of electronic coloring books (Polarware's *Electronic Crayon Series*, for example). In these programs, children use the fill tool to color in ready-made line drawings similar to those found in traditional coloring books. After thus coloring the drawings, children can print the finished product—which they generally enjoy doing—but these programs do little to develop artistic or creative skills.

Creativity—Not Just for Artists and Writers

How computer programs—other than the drawing programs or writing programs we have mentioned—foster children's creativity is another question adults who work with young children frequently ask us. It seems that with some skeptics, the computer has a drill-and-practice reputation that's hard to shake. Also, it's understandable that programs stressing creative

There are no right or wrong answers in face-creating programs, only limitless (or so it seems to the child) possibilities.

thinking are of special interest, since it is important that early childhood be a time of self-expression.

We've found computer learning activities all along the "creativity spectrum"—programs that are very open-ended, programs that are moderately open-ended, and programs that are highly focused. Many of the highly focused ones were mentioned earlier; they include programs dealing with classifying, sequencing, counting, measuring, and recognizing numerals, letters, or words. We've also mentioned ones such as the writing and drawing programs, in which children are free to determine their own focus. But there are other kinds of programs that encourage children to see "what happens if," to try different approaches, or to solve problems—in short, to be creative.

One of these is *Facemaker Golden Edition* (Spinnaker), a program that gives children the chance to create different faces by selecting eyes, ears, noses, mouths, and hairstyles from a variety of choices. Another portion of the *Facemaker* program allows a face to be programmed to smile, cry, wink, frown, or stick out its tongue in distaste, a good chance for children to explore how body language expresses emotion. After creating a face, children can print it and cut it out. There are no right or wrong answers in this program, only limitless (or so it seems to the child) possibilities. Another program that children can take in many possible directions is *Monsters and Make-Believe* (Learning Lab). Children can create monsters of their own choosing by selecting body parts from a "body shop," and then, with the help of an adult, they can dictate a ½-page story about their monster. Yet another program full of choices is *Mask Parade* (Springboard), which allows children to design and print face-masks and other cutouts, such as hats, jewelry, badges, and feet. Children find this program easy to use and like to use the cutouts for role play.

Other programs engage children in creative problem-solving activities. *Ducks Ahoy!* (Joyce Hakansson) is such a program. It is a timing and spatial-positioning game suitable for both preschool and kindergarten children. The game is set in the canals of Venice, so the computer screen shows a grid of intersecting horizontal and vertical "canals." Each square of the grid contains a house with ducks that march steadily through and out its front door. In all, there are six houses,

eight canals, and an endless supply of ducks issuing forth from each house. The child uses the joystick to control a gondola as it moves through the canals. The object of the game is to ferry ducks from their front doors to the beach. Complicating things is a hippo lurking in the canals who can spill passengers and sink the gondola.

Three- and four-year-olds playing this game in our classroom have learned quite quickly to navigate the gondolas

Children find Mask Parade *easy to use to make cutouts for their role play.*

in the grid of canals, anticipate the ducks' movements, and move the gondola to the ducks' doors to pick them up before they fall into the canal. They can also keep track of the hippo.

At first, children simply move the gondola from house to house, trying to catch ducks just as they appear at the door, but they are often unsuccessful, because the gondola is relatively small and needs to be positioned precisely to catch the ducks. The children's first step in problem solving appears to be when they learn to catch a duck by parking the gondola at one of the doors and waiting for a duck to come out (about a 10-second wait). The drawback to this strategy is that the hippo often swims in to upset the craft before it can be filled with ducks. At their highest level of problem solving, children learn to track ducks at more than one house at a time, shuttling the gondola from one house to another, catching the ducks as they appear, while simultaneously avoiding the hippo. To anticipate a duck's arrival in this manner, a child must observe the movement of several ducks and anticipate the order of their arrival at the doors.

As children problem-solve their way through *Ducks Ahoy!*, adults can talk with them about their problem-solving strategies, asking such questions as "How do you know which duck will come out next?" or "How can you get to the next duck's house without meeting the hippo?" or, as in the case of one of our High/Scope preschoolers, "Why are you helping the Hippo to overturn the boat full of ducks?" (That four-year-old had devised a different game objective and was using all his timing and predicting skills to dunk the ducks, chortling happily each time he did so!)

Other computer programs that engage children in creative problem solving are *Gertrude's Secrets* (Learning Co.), *Teddy's Playground* (Sunburst), *Ernie's Big Splash* (Hi Tech), and *Early Learning Friends* (Spinnaker).

No discussion of creativity and computers would be complete without mention of computer-programming activities; computer programming—developing, instead of following or using a developed program—is a rich arena for creative thinking. LOGO, the computer programming language for children, was designed with creative problem solving in mind. In our earlier mention of Seymour Papert's work with elementary school children and LOGO (see Chapter 1), we described how the children in Papert's lab typed coded instructions to make a robot "turtle" draw shapes and figures on the floor. Similarly, the program *EZ Logo* (MECC), intended for children four to eight years of age, entails creating sequences of commands that result in geometric patterns being drawn on the computer screen. Devising such a sequence of commands is, of course, an open-ended problem-solving task, but it requires mastery of spatial concepts and LOGO programming skill. In our experience, young children generally grasp only the simplest LOGO programming concepts. LOGO pattern design can quickly become complex (involving angles and numerical relations), and many of its programming concepts (such as sequencing, looping, and subroutines) are too difficult for preschoolers and kindergartners. LOGO does, however, illustrate the polar extreme of open-ended computer activities for young children.

Observing children as they create problem-solving strategies in computer activities impresses one with the cause-and-effect experiences that computer programs can provide.

Causality and the Computer

Observing children as they create problem-solving strategies in computer activities impresses one with the cause-and-effect experiences that computer programs can provide. Of course, learning about cause and effect—about chains of events and what controls them—is a process that starts in infancy and often isn't complete even in adulthood.

The infant's understanding of causality is self-centered. The baby who pushes a spoon to the floor to make noise or get someone's attention typically thinks of his/her desire for the sound and push of the spoon as the only causes of the results obtained.

The baby doesn't understand the forces of gravity, the physics of sound waves, or the responses of the human nervous system. Preschoolers and kindergartners likewise do not have a full understanding of changes that occur in the physical world. They often attribute life and will to inanimate objects as a way of explaining motion and change. They may, for example, believe that river water flows downhill because "it wants to reach the ocean."

Computers can help children begin to understand causality by increasing their awareness of chains of events and by helping them to separate their desire to achieve an outcome from the chain of events that leads to that outcome.

In the Lawrence Hall of Science program *Estimation* (described in Chapter 5), for example, a small train engine moving across the computer screen can be stopped by pushing the spacebar. If the train is stopped so that it's located over a spot marked with an arrow, the train whistle will toot. It's a challenging task for preschoolers and kindergartners to coordinate the position of the moving train with that of the arrow and to anticipate pressing the spacebar so the whistle will toot. Children don't understand how the computer makes the train move or how the spacebar makes it stop, but they do learn, over time, to connect the position of the arrow, the motion of the train, and the actions required to stop the train at the arrow. A similar notion of stop-and-start causality is developed as children learn to pour juice: They must learn to start the flow of juice by tipping the pitcher, then to stop it at just the right time, when the juice almost reaches the top of the cup. In both of these examples, children must coordinate complex relationships in time and space to achieve a desired end. To make something happen, they not only need to perform precise physical actions, they also need to time them correctly.

Computers can provide these kinds of cause-and-effect learning experiences because they are consistent in producing a given effect for a given cause: Whenever the train is stopped over the arrow, its whistle toots. Chil-

dren could not learn the link between cause and effect if the train only tooted some of the time when stopped over the arrow, or if the train sometimes tooted when stopped elsewhere. Some, "real-world" experiences also provide similar consistency—when the child pours juice, not stopping in time produces a mess every time— but often, real-world happenings are complex and influenced by so many factors that it's hard to discern the chain of events.

As well as providing consistency, the computer program is also completely objective in judging whether the train has been stopped in the correct spot. No matter how much a child might want the train to stop over the arrow, only the correct judgment of motion and distance will make it whistle.

It's not important for the learning of stop-and-start causality that the child understand *how* the computer makes the train stop; even most adults don't have this understanding. Rather, the computer provides the opportunity for children to learn about the movements and timing that link the position of the train with the tooting of the whistle. Thus, both computer simulations and experiences with real objects are tools available to teachers for helping children understand that physical causality involves motion, contact among physical objects, and accurate timing.

Computers and Memory Development

Problem-solving experiences and cause-and-effect experiences are not the only "fringe benefits" of computer activities. Another type of computer program that children seem to enjoy calls upon and exercises children's memory skills.

Though learning involving rote memory comes in for a lot of criticism these days, the memory process is a necessary part of almost all learning, and its role in young children's learning is often poorly understood. Remembering begins with selectively attending to and encoding information. Thus, children's ability to remember develops as they learn to notice details and to analyze and label the features of objects and experiences. Many early childhood curricula, including High/Scope's, employ strategies to help children develop these capacities for attending to and encoding their experiences.

Early childhood curricula typically include sensory awareness activities in which children work directly with objects and are encouraged to take note of and comment on their qualities: "The bark is sticky." "The bunny's fur feels fuzzy and soft." These programs also emphasize the process in which children represent their experiences through symbols and images. By helping children observe real-life similarities, differences, positions, directions, durations, and sequences, adults encourage mental representation. Adults also foster the process of mental representation by helping children produce tangible representations of their experiences (pictures, clay models, dramatic play) and by helping children plan and later recall activities. **All these representational activities help children encode experiences and thus remember them.**

Opportunities for developing children's memory skills can also be found in computer memory activities. *Memory Building Blocks* (Sunburst), *Animal Photo Fun* (DLM), and *Memory Master* (Stone), for example, contain several memory games suitable for preschool and kindergarten children. Indeed, Sunburst has published for elementary-school-aged children a series of memory-building programs including ones like *What's in a Frame?* and *Teddy and Iggy*. Though the memory content (such as recognizing which objects were presented in a previous scene or recalling the sequence of blankets on Iggy's bed) is suitable for many children of at least kindergarten age, the design of the programs in this series makes them unsuited to independent use by children who cannot read.

Concentration games, in which children find matches for hidden pictures by examining them two at a time, are another kind of memory activity frequently found in computer programs for young children. These games may actually have more value as discrimination and matching activities than as memory builders, however. *Muppetville* (Sunburst) contains concentration-style matching games for number, shape, and auditory discrimination skills. Baudville's *Rainy Day Games* contains a picture-matching concentration game (played against the computer or a partner), as well as computer versions of the children's card games Old Maid and Go Fish. The memory task of a concentration game is mostly a matter of recalling an item's spatial position, since recalling *that* an item was seen is usually easier than recalling *where* it was seen.

Computer activities such as we've described can contribute to memory development by providing tasks for practicing memory skills. **Good-quality memory tasks are those in which one or more strategies, such as noticing details, labeling, or encoding through symbols and images, can be applied by children to improve recall.** However, in most cases, adults must introduce these strategies to children as they use the programs; children do not often discover them on their own. An adult could, for example, ask a child to describe the features of objects on the screen, to say their names aloud, or to rehearse by closing the eyes and naming the objects before proceeding with the memory task. By helping children to develop such recall strategies, you will be strengthening basic thinking skills that are the foundation for subsequent learning experiences.

Learning About the Computer Itself—"Computer Literacy"

While most of this book has emphasized the use of the computer as a tool for children's learning in traditional areas—reading and writing, logical thinking, creative arts and problem solving—another possible area to consider is learning about the computer itself—its attributes, its role in our society, and its programming. This general area of direct learning about the computer is sometimes called **computer literacy**, and some educators have argued that teaching computer literacy is an essential curriculum area in our computer-oriented society. We've already expressed an opinion about exposing preschoolers and kindergartners to one facet of computer literacy— computer programming—in our discussion about LOGO. Whether

improving computer literacy in other respects is an appropriate aim for early childhood classroom activities, however, is a question we must explore. In the following paragraphs, we provide vignettes that illustrate two aspects of young children's computer literacy, and we offer our thoughts about the strengths and weaknesses of each of these potential learning areas.

Computer Attributes

In one classroom, kindergarten children have made a large model of a computer out of a range-sized cardboard box. The front of the box is decorated with circles and letters resembling a keyboard. There is also a TV screen drawn on the box, with a slot marked "input" and another marked "output." As children outside slip pieces of paper into the input slot, a child seated inside the box makes a brief drawing or writes a few letters on the paper and returns it at the output slot. The children seem aware of the major physical features of a computer, but they seem also to sense that it is a living thing, responding to their actions.

You can introduce children to the visible parts of a computer much as you would introduce them to the visible parts of a car. Young children can learn to identify the keyboard, mouse, disks, disk drive, monitor, and printer, which are often physically distinct parts of the computer. They can also learn the descriptive features of these parts—their shape, color, and function. While most of this knowledge is not essential for children's effective computer use, such learning does build children's awareness and mastery of their environment. We consider this an optional topic for early childhood classrooms.

Attempts to have preschool or kindergarten children learn the names and functions of internal parts of the computer, such as the "central processing unit" or "random access memory," are ill-conceived. Attempts to teach children about parts of the computer to which they have no direct access, at best, result in verbal knowledge without real referents. Children can derive considerable benefit from a computer without knowing more than a few of its basic features, much as adults can derive considerable benefit from an automobile without knowing more than the names and functions of the ignition, steering wheel, brakes, accelerator, and turn signals.

Many young children, when asked about their feelings towards the computer, ascribe a human, lifelike quality to it. This isn't surprising, since Piaget discovered that young children attribute lifelike qualities to running water, to moving clouds, and even to boats afloat. He found that children hold to such animistic beliefs until they are displaced by a rudimentary understanding of the mechanisms of force, resistance, and buoyancy. Be-cause a computer responds to a child's input, sends messages, computes numbers, and remembers, a child may also see the computer as a living being. Despite any adult explanations to the contrary, children's notions that the computer is alive are likely to persist for some time, until they are ready to develop greater understanding of the mechanisms of the computer.

How People Use Computers

A preschool class makes a field trip to the grocery store. On the way, they stop at a bank's automatic teller machine. After pressing some of the buttons, the teacher receives some money from the machine. Inside, children are treated to a look at the machine's computer. Later, at the supermarket, children watch as the checkout scanner reads the prices from the packages of juice and cookies they have selected; they see how numbers and words are then displayed on the checkout screen.

Children are fascinated by the machines in their world (for example, airplanes, vacuum cleaners, copying machines), and they enjoy dressing up for various adult roles and pretending they are using machines appropriate to those roles. Computers and the adults who use them as tools may likewise be fascinating to young children. Through field trips like the one described above, children can learn about the many different things computers do in their community and about the roles of adults who operate them. These experiences are valuable not only because they teach children the relevancy of computers in today's world but also because they give children a feeling of importance and power: Comparing themselves to the adults they see using computers, they realize that they too use computers in their roles as preschoolers and kindergartners.

You can see that our review of the relevance of computer literacy to early childhood classrooms is a mixed one. Some literacy will creep in of its own accord as children use the computer as a classroom tool. Other literacy will be a natural fallout of field trips into our increasingly computer-oriented communities. However, a concerted effort to produce young children who can spout "computerese" and write their own computer programs is not our recommendation. To reemphasize what we said at the outset of this book: **We view the computer not as an end in itself—a new world for children to master—but as one more tool for children to use in discovering and mastering the world of familiar experience.**

Conclusion

We began this book with some "guiding questions" about computer use in early childhood—questions about social-emotional impact, symbolic-level learning, active learning, child-initiated activity, and adult roles as they relate to computers in the classroom. In chapters describing varied uses of the computer as a learning tool, we've answered those questions with classroom examples and careful analysis of the underlying issues. In the future, the uses for this new classroom tool—the computer—are sure to expand beyond what we have described here. For example, when and if classroom computers are able to respond to human speech, preschoolers and kindergartners will have another intriguing avenue of access to language competency. Just as businesses, professions, and homes are benefiting daily from the ever-widening applications of computer technology, so will early childhood classrooms. If the new classroom applications measure favorably against the yardstick of a coherent child development theory, we can all look forward to them with enthusiasm.

Appendix: Software and Equipment Producers

Apple Computer, Inc.
20525 Mariani Avenue
Cupertino, CA 95014
408/973-3708

Baudville
5380 52nd Street S.E.
Grand Rapids, MI 49508
616/698-0888

Berkeley Softworks
2150 Shattuck Avenue
Berkeley, CA 94704
415/644-0883

Broderbund Software
17 Paul Drive
San Rafael, CA 94903
415/492-3200

CBS Software
CBS Inc., One Fawcett Place
Greenwich, CT 06836
Note: In 1987, CBS Software was dissolved. See Mindscape, Hi Tech Expressions, or Joyce Hakansson Associates, Inc., for information on old CBS titles.

C&C Software
5713 Kentford Circle
Wichita, KS 67220
316/683-6056

CLARIS Corporation
440 Cycle Avenue
Mountain View, CA 94043
408/987-7000

DLM
One DLM Park
Allen, TX 75002
800/527-4747

Edmark Corporation
P.O. Box 3903
Bellevue, WA 98009
800/426-0856
In WA, 800/422-3188

Electronic Arts
1820 Gateway Drive
San Mateo, CA 94404
415/571-7171

Hartley Courseware, Inc.
Box 419
Dimondale, MI 48821
800/247-1380
In MI, 517/646-6458

Hi Tech Expressions
Suite 9
1700 N.W. 65th Avenue
Plantation, FL 33313
800/848-9273
In FL, 305/584-6386

Houghton Mifflin Company
Educational Software Division
P.O. Box 683
Hanover, NH 03755
800/258-3545
In NH, 312/980-9710

IBM Educational Systems
P.O. Box 1328-W
Boca Raton, FL 33429
407/443-1929

Joyce Hakansson Associates, Inc.
2029 Durant
Berkeley, CA 94704
415/540-5963

Lawrence Hall of Science
University of California
Berkeley, CA 94720
415/642-3167

Learning Company, The
6493 Kaiser Drive
Fremont, CA 94555
800/852-2255

Learning Lab Software
8833 Receda Boulevard
Northridge, CA 91324
800/247-4641

MECC
Minnesota Education Computing Corporation
3490 Lexington Avenue North
St. Paul, MN 55126-8097
800/228-3504 or
612/481-3500
In MN, 800/782-0032

Mindplay
100 Conifer Hill Drive
Danvers, MA 01923
800/221-7911

Mindscape, Inc.
3444 Dundee Road
Northbrook, IL 60062
800/221-9884
In IL, 312/480-7667

Polarware, Inc.
P.O. Box 311
2600 Keslinger Road
Geneva, IL 60134
312/232-1984

PTI/Koala Industries
269 Mount Herman Road
Scotts Valley, CA 95066

Random House Software
400 Hahn Road
Westminster, MD 21157
800/638-6460
In MD, 800/492-0782
In CD, AL or HI,
   301/848-1900

Scholastic Software
730 Broadway
New York, NY 10003
800/325-6149

Simon & Schuster
200 Old Tappan Road
Old Tappan, NJ 07675
800/624-0023

Spinnaker Software Corp.
One Kendall Square
Cambridge, MA 02139
800/826-0706

Springboard
7808 Creekridge Circle
Minneapolis, MN 55435
800/445-4780 ext. 1000

Stone & Associates
Suite 319
7910 Ivanhoe Avenue
La Jolla, CA 92037
800/621-0852 ext. 520

Strawberry Hill Software
202-11961-88th Avenue
Delta, British Columbia
Canada V4C 3C9
604/594-5947

Street Electronics
6420 Via Real
Carpenteria, CA 93013
805/684-4593

Sunburst Communications, Inc.
39 Washington Avenue
Pleasantville, NY 10570
800/431-1934
In Canada, 800/247-6756

Teacher Support Software
P.O. Box 7130
Gainesville, FL 32605-7130
800/228-2871
In FL, 904/371-3802

Thirdware Computer Products
Precision Software, Inc.
4747 N.W. 72nd Avenue
Miami, FL 33166
305/592-7522

Weekly Reader Software and Optimum Resource, Inc.
10 Station Place
Norfolk, CT 06058
800/327-1473

Glossary

arrow key   Any one of four keys labeled with arrows on a computer keyboard. An arrow key can be pressed to move the on-screen cursor up, down, right, or left, depending on the direction of the arrow.

back-up copy   A copy of a computer program disk that is intended for use only if the original copy is lost or damaged.

compatible   One brand or model of a computer is compatible with another when the same programs can be run on both.

computer system   An information processing system composed of at least four parts: an input device (such as a keyboard), an output device (such as a monitor), a central processing unit (CPU), and memory. This entire system is often simply called *a computer*.

cursor   An on-screen indicator, often a small pointer or a flashing dash, that shows where the next input or output will appear on the screen.

database   A list of such information as names, addresses, or telephone numbers, often stored on disks for use with a computer.

database program   A program for organizing, sorting through, updating, and retrieving database information.

DELETE key   One or more keys used for removing text or graphic elements that are near the on-screen cursor. Possible ways that a DELETE key is indicated are by the labels "DEL" or "delete" or by a left-pointing arrow on the backspacing key.

disk drive   The mechanism into which the floppy disk or diskette is inserted. Makes the disk rotate as on a record player.

display capability   The sharpness, vividness, and complexity of the images or text that a computer can display on a TV-like screen.

dot matrix   A printed or on-screen pattern of tiny dots that forms letters, numbers, and pictures.

ENTER key   A key, often double-sized, that is used to initiate the computer's processing of newly entered information. For example, after pressing the Y or N key to indicate "yes" or "no," the user would press ENTER to initiate the processing of this response.

ESCAPE key   A key that is often used to stop the processing of a part of a computer activity and return to some starting point, such as to a menu.

file   On a computer, a set of information—such as a program or other written or graphic data—that is stored in the computer's internal memory or on a disk. A file is marked with a beginning and an end and given a unique name, so that a user can easily call it up on the screen or print it.

floppy disk   A vinyl disk, coated with magnetic material, on which computer programs can be recorded for long-term storage.

graphics   The pictorial part of a computer program presentation. (In early childhood computer programs, this includes the outsized letters and numerals that are often used.)

hard drive   A disk drive employing rigid rather than flexible (or floppy) disks. A hard disk drive generally has the capacity of hundreds of floppy disks.

hardware   See software.

HELP key   A key that is used by a program to bring needed additional information to the screen. The H key sometimes serves this function, and the Muppet Learning Keys have a special key labeled "HELP."

input   Signals sent to the computer from such a device as a keyboard, joystick, mouse, or touch pad.

joystick   A computer attachment. Movement of the joystick handle up, down, left, or right moves the on-screen cursor in corresponding directions. The joystick also has a button that may be used to stop or start action or to pick up an on-screen object.

load   To copy a program's instructions from a disk or tape into the computer's memory.

memory   The ability of a computer system to store information for later use. "Memory" can also refer to the *location* inside the computer where the information is stored.

memory capacity   The number of letters, numbers, pictures, or lines of computer instruction that the computer's memory is capable of "filing away," or storing. Usually expressed in kilobytes, or thousands of bytes: For example, a memory capacity of 64K means ability to store 64,000 bytes, which is approximately equal to 64,000 typewritten characters (more than 100 double-spaced typewritten pages).

menu   In a computer program, an on-screen list of choices for the user. For example, the list might present a choice of ways to proceed with the program, or a choice of different levels of challenge within a computer learning activity.

microcomputer   Any personal-sized computer system.

monitor   The part of a computer system that is a TV-like screen on which letters, numerals, or pictures can be displayed.

monitor, composite color   A relatively low-resolution monitor capable of displaying color images.

monitor, RGB   A relatively high-resolution monitor capable of displaying finely detailed color images. The acronym refers to the separate red, green, and blue "electron guns" involved in creating the on-screen image.

mouse   A hand-held computer attachment whose movement (left, right, up, or down) on a desk moves on-screen objects (often the cursor) in corresponding directions. The mouse also has a button that may be used to stop or start an action or pick up an object.

output   Signals sent from the computer's central processing unit to the screen or the printer.

peripheral Strictly speaking, any attachment to the computer system's central processing unit, such as a keyboard, monitor, printer, mouse, speech synthesizer, or disk drive.

port A place where peripherals for input or output are attached to the computer's central processing unit.

power pack A unit on some small computers that plugs into the wall socket and transforms the voltage from utility lines to the low-voltage electrical power required by the computer's circuits.

printer A mechanical device that prints computer output on paper.

printer hookup The cable(s) (and circuit cards, if a printer port isn't provided) needed to connect a printer to the computer system's central processing unit.

programming The writing of instructions (a program) that make a computer perform a specific task.

resolution A computer (or TV) screen's ability to clearly display fine details, such as thin lines, sharp edges and corners, and color details. For example, the resolution of present U.S. television screens is not high enough to display small letters legibly.

retrieval The process of "calling up" stored information, that is, moving stored information from disks into the computer's internal memory or from the computer's internal memory to the display screen or printer.

screen dump A copy, printed on paper or saved on a disk, of what appears on a computer screen at a given moment. Also, the peripheral (and sometimes software) required for the computer to make such a copy.

software The coded instructions that make up a computer program. Usually contrasted with the physical parts of a computer system, which are referred to as **hardware.**

speech synthesizer An output device through which letters and words are converted to speech sounds.

spreadsheet A paper form or an on-screen "form" in which data (such as numerical information) are arranged in columns and rows, as in a ledger book.

spreadsheet program A computer program designed to change, add to, work with, and retrieve spreadsheet information.

storage The "internal memory" part of a computer that files away computer programs and other information (such as words, numbers, or pictures) for later use. **Storage** can also refer to the filing away of information magnetically on a hard or floppy disk.

surge protector A device connected between the wall socket and the computer, designed to protect the computer's electrical circuits from damage due to unusual fluctuations in the power supplied by utility lines. (*Note*: To function properly, these devices nearly always require that they be plugged into properly grounded, three-prong outlets.)

telecomputing Connecting one computer with another over telephone lines.

touch pad   A touch-sensitive pad that allows information to be entered into the computer by touching selected areas on the pad. Muppet Learning Keys, the Touch Window, and the Koala Pad are touch pads.

T-switch   A switch allowing two or more computers to use a single printer or other peripheral. It may also be used to allow more than one printer to be used with a single computer.

word processing   Using a computer to type and edit text that is stored on a disk.

Index

Boldface entries are software program titles.

Database program, 51–55
Delta Drawing (Spinnaker), 79
Deluxe Paint (Electronic Arts), 93
Developmental theory. *See* Child development.
DIALOG, 55
Dictation, 63. *See also* "Language experience" stories.
Disk. *See* Floppy disk.
Disk drive, 18–19
Display capability. *See* Graphics.
Drawing, computer, 22, 89–93
Drill-and-practice, 74, 93
Dr. Peet's Talk/Writer (Hartley), 61, 63
Dr. Seuss Fix-Up the Mix-Up Puzzler (CBS), 77
Ducks Ahoy! (Joyce Hakansson), 78, 95-96

Early Learning Friends (Spinnaker), 96
Early Learning Series (Apple), 65
Easy as ABC (Springboard), 35, 67
Easy Street (Mindplay), 74
Easy Working: The Filer (Spinnaker), 55
Easy Working: The Planner (Spinnaker), 55
Easy Working: The Writer (Spinnaker), 52
Echo speech synthesizer (Street Electronics), 65
Educational Testing Service, 66–67
Electronic Crayon Series (Polarware), 93
Emergent literacy, 60–61
Emergent Literacy: Writing and Reading (Teale and Sulzby), 61
Epson computer, 20
Epson printer, 24
ERIC, 55
Ernie's Big Splash (Hi Tech), 34
Estimating, 86, 96
Estimation (Lawrence), 34, 35, 86–87, 98
EZ Logo (MECC), 79, 96

Facemaker Golden Edition (Spinnaker), 94
Fingerprint (Thirdware), 24
1st Math (Stone), 85
FirstWriter (Houghton Mifflin), 63
Fish Scales (DLM), 86
Floppy disk
care, 31, 47
drive, 18–19
Fun From A to Z (MECC), 35, 61

Gallistel, C. R., 81
Gelman, Rochel, 81
Geos FILER 64 (Berkeley), 55
Geos SwiftCALC 64 (Berkeley), 55
Geos WRITER 64 (Berkeley), 52
Gertrude's Secrets (Learning Co.), 35, 75, 96
Graphics, 5
Greater than and less than, 83, 85
Guiding questions about computers and young children, 7 ff., 102

Hardware, 15 ff. *See also* Peripherals.
choosing, 20–21
cost of, 29, 36
defined, 26
most cost-effective choice of, 21
Hess, Robert, 67
High/Scope
computer learning project, 3–5
computer training workshops, 4, 56–57
Curriculum, 3, 7 ff.
Curriculum Comparison Study, 11
demonstration classroom, 3, 44–48
key experiences, 76, 79, 81
High/Scope Survey of Early Childhood Software (Buckleitner), 7, 20, 32, 43
Home computer activities, 12–13

IBM Color Graphics printer, 23
IBM computer, 21–22, 28, 34–36, 52, 55, 67
Imagewriter II printer, 22–23
Individual use of computers, children's, 44
Information services, professional, 55
Input devices, 21, 25 ff. *See also* Peripherals.
Introducing computer activities. *See* Computer activities, introducing at group time.

Joystick. *See* Peripherals.

Keyboard skills, 28–29, 68–69
Key experiences, 76, 79, 81
Kid's Stuff (Stone), 34, 61
Kindercomp (Spinnaker), 34, 90
Kindercomp Golden Edition (Spinnaker), 34
Kindergarten software, starter set of, 33, 35 (table), 43
Koala Pad (PTI/Koala). *See* Peripherals.
Koala Pad Graphics Exhibitor (PTI/Koala), 93

Labeling, classroom and equipment. *See* Computer area.
Label making, computer, 51, 52
Laboratory approach. *See* Computer lab.
Language development
computer support of, 61 ff.
in early childhood, 60–61
Language Experience Recorder Plus (Teacher Support), 70
"Language experience" stories, 49, 69–70
Language packages
Apple Computer company, 65–66
IBM Educational Systems, 66
Large-group time, 43, 49, 69–70
Laser computer, 20, 36

Charles Hohmann,
who holds a Ph.D. in educational psychology from the University of Michigan, has coordinated preschool and elementary curriculum development at the High/Scope Foundation since 1972. During this time, he has also been involved in training elementary school teachers as part of the national Follow Through program for disadvantaged children. In addition, he directed High/Scope's Summer Workshop for Teenagers for 10 years.

Young Children and Computers is an outgrowth of Dr. Hohmann's work during the past five years studying how young children and their teachers used computers in the High/Scope demonstration classroom in Ypsilanti, Michigan. Another outgrowth of this work has been his computer training workshops for early childhood professionals throughout the United States. The positive classroom experiences of both High/Scope teachers and workshop participants have provided much of the material and inspiration for this book.